Below, is Your Reason to Read this Book

"John Lund's Vietnam 1967-1971: Danger, Affliction, Toil, Heartbreak, and Stolen Years is quite an engaging book. Lund takes us on a journey aboard the aircraft carrier Hancock on all three of his deployments on Yankee station, the Navy's designation for flight operation battle positions in the South China Sea off the coast of North and South Vietnam.

Rich with photographs and some nicely descriptive narrative, this offering-most likely unintentionally-structured like a screenplay. Lund has combed through the correspondence he shared with his bride throughout his time in the Navy and has produced a unique book.

After you get in to it, you can almost hear the intonations of Jack Webb or Peter Coyote narrating and reading the letters as the story toggles back and forth between Lund's missives to his wife and his telling of the bulk of his aboard-ship story. At times, the writing is mildly salty, but not distractingly so.

Lund begins with background on himself and his family; focusing on things and people that shaped his approach to his Navy job as a machinist mate in the engine room of the Hancock, a World War II-ear aircraft carrier pressed into service for the Vietnam War. That includes meeting his future wife in high school, one of those fable love-at-first-sight encounters.

The back cover of the book quotes Capt. Greer, the ship's commander, saying that the Hancock was "plagued with personnel shortages, inadequately trained personnel, lacked critical talent, equipment reliability that had not been assured, a long list of discrepancies, a criminally short time to marry the ship with the air wing, and with knowledge of predictable casualties." That statement forms the base for Lund's story and his subtitle, "Danger, Affliction, Toil, Heartbreak and Stolen Years.

Striving to do the best he could during his tour of duty, Lund earned letters of commendation during all three of his deployments, and rose to the post of Top Watch. His description of the engine room conditions (heat, humidity, mechanical failures, and other difficulties) make for an interesting and engaging read, even for someone who never served in the Navy. The book did need a bit more explanation of Navy lingo, though.

Returning from his third deployment, his last voyage Lund mustered out as he left the Hancock without a backward glance. As a civilian, he began experiencing medical and mental challenges that brought him face-to-face with the VA and its bureaucracy. His physical afflictions very likely were caused by frequent exposure (as many other Blue Water Navy sailors were) to Agent Orange, asbestos, and other toxic chemicals.

In the book, Lund comes across not as bitter, but surely disappointed, about it all. This was a nice read-a story well told and an enlistment well fulfilled."

—Review by Tom Werzyn
Vietnam Veterans of America

This is a compelling story. I laughed and cried. I had no idea what my brother went through during his tours of duty, and I had no idea the conditions he was subjected to.

—Carolyn Lund, author's sister

For Sandra
Forever 1966–1967
Forever Young
Forever Friends
Forever Love

Vietnam 1967–1971

Danger, Affliction, Toil,
Heartbreak, and Stolen Years

by John Lund

Printed in the United States of America

ISBN: 978-1-946195-31-9
Library of Congress Control Number: 2018968283

23 22 21 20 19   5 4 3 2 1

Photo Credits: Except for those listed below, all photos are the work of a sailor or employee of the US Navy, taken or made as part of that person's official duties. As works of the US federal government, the images are in the public domain in the United States.
Copyright John Lund and family, used with permission: 31, 33, 65, 81, 90, 92, 155, 170, 182, 187, 206, 231, 273, 288, 299 (top), 300 (top)

Cover Design & Interior Book Design: FuzionPrint

Published by FuzionPress
1250 E 115th Street, Burnsville, MN

To all those who served aboard the USS Hancock

About the Cover

This is a portrait of a young man so proud to wear the naval uniform, so proud to have served aboard a naval warship with a decorated and distinguished past, and so proud to have served his four-year tour of duty with distinction, receiving three citation letters for outstanding performance.

Today, however, the Vietnam war is considered the "greatest American disaster of the twentieth century." This knowledge adversely lingers in my mind decades after my service aboard the aircraft carrier and three deployments to a war zone.

The naval aircraft carrier appearing on the cover is the USS *Hancock*. She was deployed to Vietnam in July 1968. In December 1968 an article appeared in the Hancock *Signature*. Captain Greer wrote that the Hancock was; "plagued with personnel shortages, inadequately trained personnel, lacked critical talent, equipment reliability that had not been assured, a long list of discrepancies, a criminally short time to marry the ship with the air wing, and with knowledge of predicable casualties." His words underpin the book's title.

Contents

Preface.. 11

Introduction... 13

Politics and the Vietnam War... 19

Growing Up in Small-Town Minnesota............................ 33

Leaving Home: Boot Camp.. 47

Reporting aboard the USS *Hancock*............................. 65

February 3, 1968: Married... 83

Operation Rolling Thunder 103

Politics, War, and Arduous Life at Sea 135

The Final Months of My First Deployment 159

Stateside: 1969 189

Second Deployment to Vietnam 201

Stateside: 1970 233

My Third Deployment to Vietnam................................... 241

Returning Home: 1971 275

The Hidden Enemy 281

Final Thoughts 297

Acknowledgments... 298

About the Author 299

Preface

When working on this book, I'd retire to a quiet room, turn on music of the 1960s, and read letters I sent to my wife fifty years ago. These letters opened mental compartments—scarred mental compartments I had closed. I reopened many of those compartments with trepidation.

With only music breaking the silence within the room, I could drift back to the life of a sailor aboard a warship floating off the coast of Vietnam. As I continued to drift, the fog of past years dissipated, and my memory cleared. With my emotions provoked, I'd start writing, my words full of intense feelings—at times, anger.

I've never considered myself a writer or storyteller. So, as you read my story, I encourage you to listen to the song "Eve of Destruction," written by P. F. Sloan and performed by Barry McGuire. This outcry of the Vietnam era delivers the emotions I'm trying to convey.

For the millions who were called to service for their country, the Vietnam War left us with twisted emotions, images, and memories we tried to shut away. But now I've found that once a scarred mental compartment is opened, it's very hard to close.

Introduction

I t was the summer of 1962. I was biking the small town of Farmington, Minnesota, when my friend said a family member of his had been killed in Vietnam.

I hadn't been schooled on Vietnam nor had many adults. All we knew was that a conflict was breaking out in a land far away. We were told that our government was backing South Vietnam in an effort to stop the spread of Communism. This included sending military advisors and financial support.

I remember sitting on my bicycle seat, thinking to myself, *That conflict will be over by the time I graduate, so I won't have to worry about being killed.*

How wrong those thoughts were.

Fast-forward to 1967. The United States had ramped up its military efforts against North Vietnam, now drafting 35,000 young men per month. Those graduating from high school were concerned and worried about being sent to fight a war, a war described on the nightly news as fierce fighting sending American youth home in body bags.

It was called the Vietnam War. However, other Indo-Chinese countries and their civilian populations were drawn into the war as several United States presidents directed a campaign against Communism. This campaign would have deadly consequences with deaths in the millions.

This book chronologically weaves the struggles of a very young man who enlisted in the navy before he graduated from high school in 1967, got engaged before he left for boot camp, married at age eighteen before deploying to Vietnam, and became both a war veteran and a father at age nineteen. Before his twenty-first birthday, he achieved the rank of an E-

5 noncommissioned officer. As a petty officer second class, he was responsible for the operation, repair, and maintenance of the Number 3 and 4 ship service turbo generators, served as M Division's section leader, and qualified as top watch in the forward and aft engine rooms.

Mature, street-smart, gritty, full of integrity, focused, driven, respected, and respectful—this young man was determined to serve at the highest level for the mission of his country. He received three letters of citation from the ship's captain for outstanding performance during each deployment to Vietnam.

Most of all, this young man was determined to succeed for Sandra, the love of his life.

USS Hancock *(CVA-19)*

From July 1968 through June 1971, I served on three combat deployments with the USS *Hancock* (CVA-19), a World War II aircraft carrier. The picture is of the *Hancock* leaving for deployment with the Golden Gate Bridge in the background. My emotions when viewing this photo are profound! There's honor, having served in the United States Navy with distinction aboard a warship with a distinguished history. There's also heartbreak, remembering my separation from my wife, Sandra.

Sandra and I wrote most everyday while I was deployed overseas. She kept my letters, and fifty years later, they became my diary and road map for this book—from my first day in boot camp, to my service aboard the *Hancock* during combat operations off the coast of Vietnam, to my honorable discharge from the United States Navy on June 2, 1971. These letters brought to life memories of a bygone era, memories that float between affliction, toil, heartbreak, and stolen years.

Be advised that what you are about to read is written with a sailor's vocabulary. There will be jargon and expressions that were spoken in the bowels of a World War II naval ship deployed during the Vietnam War. It's not written in a warm and congenial tone. At times, it is bold, raw, and R-rated to convey my story and the emotions I've captured in the book's title.

You'll read about moments that were funny as well as moments that were infuriating and disgusting. You'll also read about life-threatening events and death. And intertwined in these moments, I'll describe four years of separation from the woman I fell in love with before entering the military. My three combat deployments caused heartache, pain, and—even today—sorrow.

In this book, I'll provide insight into life aboard a military ship, including the irresponsible, indecent, and illicit lifestyle most sailors experienced in foreign ports. It was an abyss for me as an eighteen-year-old to navigate and a snake hole that swallowed up many of my peers.

In March 2018, I toured the USS *Lexington* museum. The *Lexington* was a sister ship to the *Hancock*. The exhibits show sailors neatly clothed, smiling, serving delicious food, and living in an atmosphere of well-being. Those mock-ups do not reflect reality.

I know the true reality. Understand, my first two and a half years in the navy were a bitch! The ship's crew was pushed to the limit, as was the old carrier itself. That combination was a recipe for disaster. The military worked my ass off in extremely harsh conditions, put me in harm's way, fed me powdered shit mixed with water and called it food—all for a few self-serving and deceitful political leaders.

This narrative also includes information about heroes who were killed during the Vietnam War, who made the ultimate sacrifice for the United States. Give pause—for these are heroes no longer with their families. They're each someone's son, husband, brother, father, daughter, sister, wife, or mother. Their families each heard a knock on the door, only to find military personnel in dress uniform verbalizing gut-wrenching news that their loved one had been killed and when the casket would arrive in the United States. Or worse, that the body had been lost at sea and there would be no closure.

Of those not killed, many suffered laborious, life-threating conditions, and many came home with mental and physical scars that linger today. I can't stress this point enough. In fact, I provide a crude image in chapter 14 to illustrate my point. Hopefully, each reader will understand that our veterans' suffering continues today!

This book is more than just a memoir, though. This narrative also exposes how dishonest and self-serving American leaders stole the youthful years of tens of thousands of young American men. In this book, I use harsh and damming words to express discontent for US leaders in the 1960s. They tore eighteen-year-olds from their families and the fabric of their communities, then sent them ten thousand miles away to fight in a war established by deceit.

As a young sailor, I did not question the United States' stance on the Vietnam War, and I served my country with honor. I'm proud of the medals, ribbons, and three letters of citation I was awarded. But today, something doesn't feel right. Why? I served my country with honor, and my military record demonstrates my commitment. But I also feel like a member of a team that lost the Super Bowl yet was still awarded the trophy. I served in a war that the world's greatest superpower lost to an army of mostly peasants—embarrassing.

Revisiting a war that occurred fifty years ago—it's painful. There's a pit in my stomach as I open old mental compartments I had tightly closed when I walked off the ship's gangplank for the last time on June 2, 1971. I struggle knowing that the efforts of those who served, those who were injured, and those who died for the United States were in vain.

In the 1960s, the public viewed those serving in the United States military as part of the Vietnam problem. At times, military personnel were vilified. At least that's the way it felt walking through the airport in uniform. Today, though, many strangers who see my Vietnam hat will walk up, shake my hand, and say the words, "Thank you for your service." It is very much appreciated by all veterans.

I'm a war survivor who served his country with honor and distinction. And by the grace of God, I returned home to my wife, raised a family, and watched my grandchildren grow.

This is my story. And this is the story of the Vietnam War.

Chapter 1

Politics and the Vietnam War

President Lyndon B. Johnson signing the Gulf of Tonkin Resolution (H.J. RES 1145), passed by Congress

After enlisting in the United States Navy and completing boot camp, I received military orders to report aboard an aircraft carrier deployed during the Vietnam War. I served with an understanding, as portrayed by the US government, that the war was a just cause. In reality, we now understand that millions of American youth were commandeered by deceitful leaders to fight in a worthless and immoral war that the United States lost. Before I can tell my own story, it's important to understand the truth behind this war.

The Political Path to War

Starting with Harry S. Truman after WWII and continuing with Dwight D. Eisenhower and John F. Kennedy, each president ramped up the conflict against Communism little by little. This was in line with the Truman Doctrine, which implied American support for nations threatened by Communism. The United States quietly funded this cause with American taxpayers' hard-earned dollars and—worst of all—the lives of the American youth.

The Vietnam War was a conflict that occurred in the Indo-Chinese countries of Vietnam, Laos, and Cambodia from 1954 to 1975, with involvement from active US combat units beginning in 1965. It was officially fought between North Vietnam and the government of South Vietnam. The North Vietnamese Army was supported by the Soviet Union, China, and other Communist allies. South Vietnam was supported by the United States, Australia, South Korea, and other anti-Communist allies. The Vietcong, a mass political organization in South Vietnam, was a Communist common front aiding North Vietnam and fighting the anti-Communist forces in the region. North Vietnam and the Vietcong were fighting to reunify Vietnam. The United States viewed involvement in the war as a way to prevent the Communist takeover of South

Vietnam and the potential spread of Communism via the domino theory.

As time progressed, the Central Intelligence Agency (CIA), directed by the White House, carried out secret military operations against Communist North Vietnam and the Vietcong. In August 1964, President Johnson informed the American public that North Vietnamese gunboats attacked and exchanged shots with the USS *Maddox*, a destroyer, in the Gulf of Tonkin. He accused the North Vietnamese of "open aggression on the high seas"—remember those words. He used this attack to rally the United States Congress into passing the Gulf of Tonkin Resolution, which gave him, as commander in chief, the power to take all necessary measures in what then became an undeclared war.

However, what he didn't tell the American public and Congress was that he had been provoking North Vietnam prior to the attack on the USS *Maddox*. Understand, if you keep poking someone in the eye, you'll eventually anger your adversary and incite a reaction. Americans had no idea Johnson had been itching to escalate the conflict into an undeclared war and used the Gulf of Tonkin incident to do just that.

That year, Johnson was running for reelection against Senator Barry Goldwater. Even though Johnson was secretly escalating the war, his campaign promised a tough stance to deescalate it. At an October 1964 campaign stop in Akron, Ohio, Johnson said to the American people, "We are not about to send American boys nine or ten thousand miles from home to do what Asian boys ought to do for themselves."

Johnson's deceit appeased the voters with his display of verbal optimism and assurances that American boys would not be sent to Vietnam. He was sworn in as president on January 20, 1965. Well, guess what? In September 1968, my ass ended up in Vietnam, ten thousand miles from my home in Minnesota!

One of the voters he appeased was my dad. Dad was a Democrat, past chairman of the Democratic Party in Chippewa County and once a candidate for state senator in Minnesota District 17. He knew Johnson, actually. In the early 1960s, he met then Texas senator Johnson and Minnesota senator Hubert H. Humphrey in Washington to lobby for railroad unions. My dad believed the president's rhetoric—many Americans did. In the 1960s, the American public simply believed that their government was telling the truth.

It didn't take Johnson long to turn on his empty campaign promises. He held a press conference on July 28, 1965, saying he would send forty-four combat battalions to Vietnam. This increased the presence to 125,000 men. Johnson then stated, "I do not find it easy to send the flower of our youth, our finest young men, into battle. . . . I know, too, how their mothers weep and how their families sorrow." This was a mouthful of hollow words manipulating the emotions of the American public!

Johnson did more than lie and deceive the American people. As history has confirmed without a doubt, he also wasted our country's blood and treasure. His administration's strategy for and prosecution of the Vietnam War left our finest young boys in harm's way, injured, and dead.

Johnson and Secretary of Defense Robert McNamara greatly distrusted the Joint Chiefs of Staff's military knowledge and advice. So Johnson and McNamara self-directed the war from the White House, putting personal, national, and international politics over military strategy. Sitting in their easy chairs, leaning back with cigarettes hanging out of their lips, they debated the war and worried about their next political move for personal gain, giving themselves an intellectual testosterone moment—my words.

Then in 1967, McNamara read the Pentagon Papers, a top-secret report he commissioned on the Vietnam War. The report detailed a war that couldn't be won. In November 1967, McNamara submitted a memorandum to Johnson recommending the United States freeze its troop levels, cease the bombing of North Vietnam, and turn over responsibility for fighting the ground war to the South Vietnamese. Johnson rejected these recommendations outright; McNamara resigned. As irritated as he was, Johnson knew McNamara was correct.

I believe this was why Johnson announced in the spring of 1968 that he would not run for reelection that fall. Instead, Hubert Humphrey, vice president at the time, ran on the Democratic ticket against Republican nominee Richard Nixon. They were locked in a tight race.

As the election neared, Johnson made progress with the Paris peace talks, which aimed to negotiate a settlement between the US, North Vietnam, and South Vietnam. By that point, half a million American military personnel were in the war zone, and more than 30,000 had already died.

To show good faith, Johnson halted the bombing campaign known as Operation Rolling Thunder on October 31. This brought North Vietnam to the table. However, South Vietnam backed away, and negotiations broke down. Consequently, Nixon defeated Humphrey on November 5.

Nixon's Treason

As it turned out, Nixon had played politics with the lives of the American youth in order to win the presidency. He had set up a secret back channel to send a message that the South Vietnamese government should withdraw from the peace talks, refuse Johnson's deal, and hold out for a much better deal once Nixon was, presumably, elected.

In recent years, many resources about the Vietnam conflict have been declassified, including audio tapes and fifty million pages of documents that detail how Nixon—acting merely as a presidential candidate and not an elected official—sabotaged the peace negotiations. This was an act of treason for Nixon's own benefit. It violated the Logan Act of 1799, which prohibits any interference by American citizens with negotiation of the United States government.

But while we Americans were not aware of Nixon's treasonous acts back in 1968, Johnson was. In a phone conversation days after the election, Johnson put Nixon on notice. "They're killing Americans every day," Johnson said. He added, "I have that documented," referring to the evidence he had on Nixon.

And the worst of it all? After everything he did to scuttle the peace talks, Nixon was ultimately unable to give South Vietnam a better deal. So the war continued, even after Nixon was sworn in as president on January 20, 1969. Tens of thousands of American youth would continue to encounter arduous conditions, danger, injury, and death.

As one who served in the war, I realize that serving as a pawn for a legitimate cause is one thing. But serving as pawn for an individual who committed treason for his own self-interest is unforgiveable!

Nixon also went on to make another secret negotiation, this time with North Vietnam in 1970. Nixon authorized his national security advisor Henry Kissinger to secretly negotiate with North Vietnam to push back the end of the war by fifteen months to ensure Nixon's reelection in 1971. This despicable act continued the injury and death of American youth. The US lost the war; 58,318 young Americans died; tens of thousands of American youth were injured, with most still suffering today; over three million South Vietnamese, North Viet-namese, Laotians, and Cambodians died; and the South Vietnamese and Cambodian people experienced a crushing defeat and suffered unimaginable consequences after the US walked away in 1975. Oh, by the way, Kissinger was given the Nobel Peace Prize for his negotiating skills.

In 1971, military analyst Daniel Ellsberg leaked the Pentagon Papers, exposing the real truths of the Vietnam War. Nixon accused him of treason—ironic, given Nixon's own traitorous acts. Nixon even authorized unlawful acts against Ellsberg to discredit him. Nixon had no conscience and played politics with the lives of American youth!

It gripes my ass when people say we need to look at all the good Nixon did. We should not have exempted him from full condemnation and punishment for his actions. President Gerald Ford was wrong to pardon Nixon for Watergate, and Johnson was wrong to withhold Nixon's 1968 act of treason from the American public. Johnson just wanted to leave himself a trump card against Nixon, and Nixon knew this. The phrase politicians like to use is "for the better interest of our country." Really!

Failed Leadership

As a Vietnam veteran who served under Johnson and Nixon, I ask that you please don't challenge my position and emotions with positive statements about either of these presidents. Otherwise, be ready for an aggressive response. These two presidents deceived the American public, mismanaged the Vietnam War via politics, and discounted military advice and planning from their four-star generals and admirals. Both administrations ignored the advice of their Joint Chiefs of Staff, which resulted in a failed war with ten years of injury and death for American youth.

Our senior military leaders were schooled at West Point and Annapolis and were seasoned veterans of WWII and the Korean War. They warned that never again should a land war be fought in this area of the world—unless tactical nuclear weapons could be deployed. Tactical nuclear weapons could take out the opposing political leadership from the top down; take out the military leadership; cut off all supply of food, fuel, and ammo; and cut off the money trails. Collateral damage to civilians must be accepted.

Yes, it's a pragmatic, harsh approach. But it's war. It's you or me. It's our youth or your civilians.

However, neither the Johnson nor Nixon administrations had the intestinal fortitude and mental courage to make the difficult decisions to win the war—my words. Our government didn't have the mettle to do what was necessary to achieve victory. If our presidents couldn't stomach the consequences of combat needed to win the war, then they shouldn't have sent our young men and women to fight a war they, as leaders, weren't willing to win.

Every war must be prosecuted to win swiftly and with minimal loss of US blood and treasure. Politics and self-interest of those holding government offices be dammed—or let their sons and daughters be the first to serve on the front lines of death.

In contrast, North Vietnam and the Vietcong didn't have a breaking point. They wouldn't negotiate for anything less than full control over a Communist South Vietnam. They were prepared to be obliterated—wiped off the face of the earth. Two presidential administrations chose not to recognize this.

And so Johnson and Nixon managed to lose what was a humiliating and destructive war against an army of peasants. During our ten-year military commitment to support South Vietnam, our tactical nuclear weapons remained on the shelf while we sustained large losses in men, money, and material—all nonrecoverable.

Our officials refused to use tactical nuclear weapons, yet they also knew land missions were failing with growing discontent and resentment of the ground troops. So our leaders settled for an ineffective bombing campaign instead. During the entire Vietnam War, the United States flew three million sorties and dropped nearly eight million tons of bombs—four times the tonnage dropped during all of World War II. It was the largest display of firepower in the history of warfare. I witnessed this firepower firsthand, as sorties were flown most every day during my three combat deployments to Vietnam.

Ken Hughes of the University of Virginia's Miller Center argues with a great deal of evidence that the bombing was chiefly designed so Nixon would win reelection. Journalist Bob Woodward cites Hughes in stating that "the massive bombing did not do the job militarily, but it was politically popular." As I write about the injuries and deaths of pilots serving aboard the USS *Hancock* in the chapters to follow, keep in mind the quote above.

As you read my narrative, please also give thought to these words from Bob Woodward:

> *President Nixon's myth of a "victory" in Vietnam masks cowardice for political courage and replaces patriotism with opportunism. Nixon prolonged a lost war. He then faked a peace. And he then schemed to shift the blame onto Congress. If the truth is masked, other presidents can play politics with lives of*

hundreds of thousands innocent civilians, and tens of thousands of American soldiers.

For years, our presidents repeatedly declared that we could not tolerate the loss of Southeast Asia to Communism and that the war was vital to our country's interests, prestige, and security. They handed the American public a glass of Kool-Aid. The character of those two leaders does not raise much above that of cult leader Jim Jones.

Discontent among the Troops

The US was fighting a peasant army—and losing. Yes, that was largely because the war was ill managed. But it was also due to the fact that our young military force was littered with drug usage, racial turmoil, and rabid dissention and discontent. Colonel Robert D. Heinl Jr. said it best in June 1971: "Our army that now remains in Vietnam is in a state approaching collapse, with individual units avoiding or having refused combat, murdering their officers and noncommissioned officers, drug-ridden, and dispirited where not near mutinous."

Prior to the Vietnam War, the US military was considered at its best. However, as the Vietnam War ramped up and dragged on, there was a sharp decline in morale and discipline among the troops. From 1967 to January 1972, 354,000 military personnel either deserted or were reported as absent without leave (AWOL). It became an epidemic. In other cases, personnel refused to follow orders, committing unauthorized stand-downs and outright sabotage. Because of rampant ground troop resistance and sabotage, the White House had to switch primarily to an air war.

Discontent and sabotage plagued the navy as well. The

following are a few of the ships that were affected:

- USS *Anderson*: nuts and bolts were dropped into the reduction gears
- USS *Ranger*: a paint scraper and two twelve-inch bolts were dropped into the Number 4 main engine reduction gears
- USS *Forestall*: a massive fire swept through the admirals' quarters and radar center
- USS *Constellation*: the captain feared mutiny of his ship and returned to San Diego to regain personnel control

In the fall of 1971, the crew of the USS *Coral Sea* started a "Stop Our Ship" (SOS) petition to prevent the ship from taking an active part in the war. The SOS movement spread to other attack aircraft carriers, including the USS *Hancock* and the USS *Ranger*.

As I look back, I believe there were three reasons for the SOS campaign: One, the ships were only stateside for five months and deployed a minimum of eight months, causing much toil and heartbreak. Two, during those long deployments, sailors suffered terrible working conditions, terrible living conditions, terrible food, long hours, dangerous conditions, and more. Three, and worst of all, sailors had to deal with officers such as Mr. Schmuck, about whom you will read.

However, even with those hardships, the majority of the ships' crews served the mission with an oath of duty and honor, sworn to upon entering military service. Wrongful acts such as sabotage went against not only the United States of America but also those with whom you served. Sabotage could cause harm, injury, and even death. There was no justification.

This discontent between non-rates and officers spiraled

into the great tragedy of "fragging." Fragging was slang for the murder of an officer or noncommissioned officer (NCO) at the hands of a disgruntled US soldier. In particular, many of these murders were committed via a fragmentation grenade. It is believed that at least eight hundred officers and NCOs died by fragging in Vietnam. One of my own best friends was a victim of fragging, which I discuss in chapter 8.

In some cases, bounties of $50 to $1,000 were placed on officers and NCOs. A bounty of $10,000 was placed on Lieutenant Colonel Weldon Honeycutt, the officer who ordered and led the attack on Hamburger Hill.

There was a possible fragging incident on the *Hancock* during my second deployment. The ship had been on the line for a couple of weeks when a first-class petty officer from another division went missing. He was never found. Scuttlebutt was, he was thrown overboard one night.

Desertion, sabotage, and fragging weren't the only results of the troops' dissent. Drug use was rampant in the military. Nearly 80 percent of troops experimented with marijuana, opium, or heroin, which were all easy to obtain on the streets of Saigon. By the end of 1971, over 30 percent of the combat troops were on smack.

These numbers are staggering. Understand—many military personnel were high on drugs during combat operation both on land and at sea. I believe this must have had a direct effect on the mission and on injuries and casualties. Think of how it jeopardized the military's mission and put troops in harm's way.

During my time in the navy, I saw firsthand how drugs became more prevalent—and how the navy went soft on use. In November 1967, just after I had reported to the *Hancock* for the first time, a machinist's mate got caught with a small amount of marijuana in his locker. He was court-martialed and given a dishonorable discharge. No second chance. A year and half later, however, anyone caught with marijuana was only busted down a rank and maybe saw brig time. But the navy did not kick them out. That's because there was a shortage of qualified navy personnel to fill the ship's billets. The navy had to manage its losses.

Danger, Affliction, Toil, Heartbreak, and Stolen Years

This was a war of broken spirits, broken hearts, lost comrades, lost friends, and lost family. Our trusted elected leaders not only served us verbal Kool-Aid but outright lied to us. The wound is deep, and it doesn't take much to scratch off the scab. Thousands of our high school graduates were sacrificed for a lost cause. Eighty percent of those who died in Vietnam were between the age of seventeen and twenty-one.

Fifty years later, we now know Vietnam was:

- a war of continuous error and misjudgment by US presidents and their administrations
- a war President Johnson promised would be fought by Vietnamese, not American, youth
- a war dogged by politics
- a war where President Johnson and his defense secretary—the ex-CEO of Ford Motor Company—didn't heed the military advice of the Joint Chiefs of Staff
- a war planned and continued to aid the reelections of both Johnson and Nixon
- a war so adverse, it had negative effects on our military forces on land, at sea, and in the air

- a war military personnel refused to fight at times
- a war laden with discrimination that impeded the ability to carry out the mission on numerous occasions
- a war where a third of the military force was on drugs, further hampering the mission
- a war where the military force began killing its own noncommissioned and commissioned officers, a practice called "fragging"
- a war so stricken with internal personnel problems and failing land missions that the White House had to refocus on fighting with air power
- a war the warriors in the field realized they were losing—a fact overlooked or ignored by those in the White House

For those of us fortunate to make it home, many are still scarred mentally and physically—all for a flawed war that was worthless and that served little purpose. If the United States wonders why so many Vietnam veterans struggle, it's because they realize they were military pawns for two presidents.

As you continue now with my own personal story, please understand this: *Our politicians—not the military rank and file—lost the Vietnam War.* In the following chapters, I share how my early years set the table for my four years of achievement and success in the United States Navy and how my experience aboard a combat ship during a war corroborates the book's title.

Chapter 2

Growing Up in Small-Town Minnesota

1963 antique tractor show, a favorite summer outing

Born in 1949, I grew up around mechanical equipment, farm machinery, cars, and tractors, all of which set the table for my success in the navy. My oldest brother, Olaf, was a machinist's mate in the navy. For that reason, I had always wanted to follow in his footsteps.

I was nine years younger than Olaf, and he mentored me on the operation of farm machinery from a young age. At the time, our family had forty acres of farmland in Montevideo, Minnesota. I remember sitting between Olaf's legs on a tractor at a very young age as he plowed our uncle's cornfield, which was also in Montevideo. It was a chilly fall night, and we had the tractor lights on. This is an experience I can still visualize today.

Olaf owned a black 1949 Ford with a standard transmission, his first car. I remember when Dad brought it home for Olaf and drove it into the yard. It was a sharp-looking car. Then before Olaf left for the service, he also bought my aunt and uncle's 1953 Oldsmobile with an automatic transmission.

Once when Olaf was home on leave from the navy, his Ford wouldn't start due to a dead battery. He said, "John, I need a push to start the Ford." So, I hopped in the Olds, and he hopped in the Ford. I matched up our bumpers and pushed him down our long gravel drive, then made a left turn onto the Wegdahl Road. I pushed him to a speed of about fifteen miles per hour, and he released the clutch on the Ford. The engine turned over several times and then started. He accelerated and pulled away from me. Now that he had the engine running, we turned the cars around and drove back to the farm.

I was nine years old and not very tall. I had to pull myself up to the steering wheel so I could see over the top and out the front window. I was just barely able to reach the gas and brake pedals.

The summer before my sixth-grade year, I remember driving a farm tractor from my uncle's farm near Watson, Minnesota, through the town of Montevideo to my dad's farm. My point is, if it had a steering wheel, I wanted to drive it.

Dad was a conductor on the railroad. He gained union seniority to hold the position of a branch-line conductor serving Farmington, Minnesota, and adjacent small towns. This meant he worked days and was home every night and weekends—a family-oriented life. So, Dad and Mom sold their farm in Montevideo and moved the family to Farmington, where I would attend sixth grade.

The summers before my ninth- and tenth-grade years, I lived with my uncle Ray and my aunt Ada on their farm in Watson, helping with their farmwork. They were good people, and I have fond memories. Uncle Ray had a 1937 Dodge pickup—four cylinders with a three-speed standard transmission. I woke up every morning hoping I'd get a chance to drive it.

Uncle Ray was the oldest of my uncles, born in 1905. He was easy to work for and not one to give a lot of verbal instruction. I learned by watching and mimicking his methods and techniques of operating farm equipment. It was a continuous learning experience of driving tractors, hauling grain and hay, spreading manure, and completing other farming chores. I didn't realize it at the time, but this was "on-the-job training."

1937 Dodge, though Uncle Ray's didn't look quite this nice!

My uncle's farm was situated in a beautiful river valley. To leave the valley, you'd take a long gravel road, go up a slight incline to cross a set of railroad tracks, then proceed up a winding road on a steep hill.

Early in the summer of 1963, Uncle Ray was pulling a load of chicken manure up this hill so he could spread it on the eighty acres he owned at the top of the hill. I was standing on the rear axle and hanging on to the fender of his Fordson Major diesel tractor as he drove. I watched his every move. On the long road before the hill, he had the tractor in sixth gear with the high-low shift lever in high range. We were moving at top speed—about fifteen miles per hour—as we approached the hill.

We crossed the railroad tracks, then continued up the steep, winding road. The diesel engine started to smoke as the revolutions per minute (rpm) dropped. The engine labored, and the tractor slowed. The heavy load of manure challenged the engine as the rpm continued to drop. The exhaust was now smoking jet black. Even though I wasn't driving, I was still excited.

I could hear the engine rpm pull down to a point where it would stall if Uncle Ray didn't downshift to a lower gear. Just then, he quickly disengaged the clutch with his right foot and shifted the high-low lever to low, dropping the transmission to a lower gear. Changing the gear ratio by 50 percent increased the engine's rpm and torque, allowing the tractor to pull the heavy load to the top of the hill.

A couple of weeks later, there was another load of manure to spread on the acreage at the top of the hill. Uncle Ray told me I could spread this load by myself. I was excited. I loved to drive the diesel tractor.

I did exactly as he did. I was in sixth gear, high range—max speed—as I crossed the railroad tracks and started up the steep hill. About a third of the way up the hill, the tractor started to slow, the rpm dropped, and the exhaust started smoking black.

I still wasn't very tall. So when the moment came to downshift, I had to stand up and disengage the clutch with my right foot, shift the high-low lever down with my right hand, yet still steer with my left hand. Luckily, I didn't miss the shift. If I hadn't properly timed my shift with the sound of the engine's rpm dropping, I would have stalled it, and the tractor would have gone backward down the hill and crashed in the ditch—not good.

But once I made the shift, the tractor continued to smoke black as the rpm increased. The tractor slowly gained speed and powered its way to the top of the hill. It was a pure adrenaline rush!

When I got back to the farmyard with the tractor, Uncle Ray said in a monotone voice, "Next time you go up the hill with or without a load, shift down to first gear." I was like a sponge with this method of learning, which I excel at, and I was in an environment I enjoyed.

In February 1965, the winter of my tenth-grade year, I turned sixteen—old enough to get a real job. But first, I needed a driver's license. I had passed my driver's permit test, but I couldn't yet take the road test for my actual license. In the 1960s, a highway patrol officer administered your behind-the-wheel road test. And in Farmington, they only did it on Wednesdays during school hours. But the school district wouldn't allow you to miss class for the test. (Heaven forbid, you might miss out on reading *Romeo and Juliet*.) So it seemed I had to wait until summer to take my test.

But then the stars lined up for me. One Wednesday, Farmington had a snowstorm that caused them to close school. Seeing an opportunity, I asked Dad if I could take my driver's test. He said, "Sure." He parked the car at the highway patrol office before he walked to work. The train depot was only three blocks from our house and two blocks from the patrol office.

At nine o'clock, I walked over to the highway patrol office through the blowing snow, opened the door, and asked the officer if I could take my driver's test. I remember him looking at me like, "Are you *crazy*?"

"I'm not pushing you out if the car gets stuck in the snow," he said.

"Okay," I replied.

I went out to start the car and clean off the snow. Dad's car was a white 1961 Oldsmobile 98—a big, heavy car with rear-wheel drive and snow tires. Soon the officer came out and got into the car. He gave me instructions, then off we went into the blowing snow with the windshield wipers on full speed.

I remember pulling up to the parallel-parking flags. I backed the car up in between the three flags with no problem. I never spun the tires!

The officer opened his door to check to see how close I was to the curb. The snow was so deep he couldn't see the curb.

"You pass," he said, even though I hadn't finished the full test. "Let's go back to the office."

I remember driving the car home with a smile on my face. I had my driver's license.

The summer of 1965, I worked for several farmers, including the Fair Hills Farm in Farmington. I baled hay, hauled grain, and spread manure. The upside—I was in my glory with a steering wheel in my hands—I loved driving tractors and working on a farm. If there was a downside, it would be that farming out in the elements is very physical work. Loading and unloading hay bales in full sun and ninety-plus-degree heat was the norm. But I loved it.

I was thankful for the early knowledge I had gained from my dad's and my brother's mentoring and my early experience working on my uncle's farm driving tractors and pulling equipment. Building on those skills, I also learned how to take orders and work under the direction of someone I didn't know. Again, I didn't realize it was great training for the navy.

The fall of 1965, I was in eleventh grade. I was hired by the Rambler dealership in Farmington to prep new cars for delivery and trade-ins for resale. This job had a lot of steering wheels!

Mr. H., the owner, was a straitlaced Bible-thumper. He was easygoing, but he demanded no swearing, no disrespect, and no false statements. He expected his employees to be pleasant to his customers. That was not a problem for me. I learned a lot from Mr. H. and applied it over the next several years. He was a great boss, and I have a lot of great memories.

Mr. H. liked to have fun, and that meant drag-racing his used cars and clients' cars. His only direction was to not leave rubber marks on the car lot's asphalt when we took off from a dead stop. Seeing tire marks all over a car lot would send most customers away. No one wanted to buy cars that appeared to have been abused or beat.

One Saturday, Mr. H. and I went out to his brother's home in the country to retrieve an old orange single-axle dump truck Mr. H. owned. We jumped the battery to start the truck, then Mr. H. told me I could drive it back to his dealership. The truck had a big steering wheel and a four-speed transmission with a two-speed rear end. I was in hog heaven.

Pulling out of the driveway, I didn't need long to realize this old dump truck had no brakes. Yet somehow I had to drive it through the town of Farmington. I had to double-clutch the transmission to lower gears to slow down, and then I had to shut the key off to come to a stop—crazy!

Back at the dealership, I went up to Mr. H. "That truck has no brakes!" I said.

He just laughed. "We'll have to bleed them," he said. He had known all along it didn't have any brakes—the laugh was on me.

He wouldn't get the last laugh, though.

About a month or so later, Mr. H. asked if I could work late. He needed help taking several cars up to the auction block in Minneapolis. At 8:00 p.m. he closed the dealership, and our caravan left for Minneapolis. I was driving a 1958 Oldsmobile Rocket 88 with a 371-cubic-inch engine and a four-barrel carburetor. Mr. H. was driving a 1958 Pontiac with a 389-cubic-inch engine and a four-barrel carburetor. His nephew was driving a 1960 Dodge with a Slant 6 engine. His brother brought up the rear in a new Rambler station wagon to commute us all back to the dealership.

Mr. H. had a heavy foot. We were cruising on Highway 3 above the speed limit. His nephew blew the transmission in the Dodge trying to keep up with Mr. H. and myself, so he left the Dodge alongside the road and caught a ride with his dad in the Rambler.

When we came to our first set of four-lane stoplights, Mr. H. stuck his hand out his window and motioned for me to pull next to him, so I did. I knew he wanted to drag from light to light. I also knew the Pontiac he was driving had a broken motor mount on the left side of the engine. That meant full acceleration caused excessive twist to the 389 engine, which pulled the throttle linkage forward and held the gas pedal to the floor. The only way to stop the acceleration was to turn the key off. I had experienced this problem during a test drive a week or so earlier, when I was prepping the car for resale.

Now as we waited at the stoplight, I power-braked the Oldsmobile. Then the light turned green. We both jammed the gas pedals to the floors, creating a light squeal of the rear tires. These were big, heavy cars. They weren't the fastest—but they were fun. I can still see the smile on his face as we were running even with each other.

I can also still see the oh-shit look on his face when the next light turned yellow and his gas pedal stayed nailed to the floor even when he took his foot off. He ran right through the red light and finally turned the key off to come to a stop.

Later, he said to me, "I couldn't slow down!"

I smiled. "Oh, I forgot to tell you about the broken motor mount." This time, it was my turn to laugh, and he knew it.

During a severe ice storm in February 1964, Dad was given an order to deliver railroad cars to a city via an overpass. But he feared the ice was so thick on the rail tracks that it would cause the engine to derail at the top of the overpass. Dad refused to comply with the order, even though his supervisor threatened him with termination. (A threat he didn't follow through on.)

Later that day, Dad needed to redirect his train via a manual rail switch. But while he was straining to muscle the switch, he slipped and broke his back.

Dad stayed home the next day with a serious back injury. The next day, the conductor filling in for Dad was given the same order to route the train via the overpass, and he complied. As the train engine reached the top of the overpass, the thick ice caused it to derail. The engine fell off the overpass to the road below.

Dad worked for the Milwaukee Railroad for over twenty years and had experienced many severe winter storms in Minnesota. He understood the effects a winter storm could have on his train. Empirical knowledge is priceless!

After Dad had back surgery at the Mayo Clinic, the railroad retired him. So the spring of my eleventh-grade year,

Dad and Mom bought a small resort in Lake City, Minnesota. I finished the school year in Farmington, then we moved to Lake City, where I would attend my senior year of high school.

I was offered a job that summer driving tractor, pulling pea combine. It would have been twelve-hour days, seven days per week, but it would have paid a very good wage. I think it would have been a gratifying job. These were big tractors with lots of power, pulling big machinery. But Mom wanted me to stay home that summer and help Dad with the outside work, which I did.

As I look back, this was the best year of my life. That summer, I met Dave, who was also going to be a senior at Lincoln High School in the fall of 1966. I hung around with Dave during the summer months, joining a car club and making friends with other local teenagers.

When school started, Dave introduced me to Sandra Ramboldt. I still remember the moment. It was the first week of school, noon hour, full sun. Dave and I were just about to enter the main door of the high school when he saw Sandra and stopped her to introduce us to each other. She was beautiful—long brown hair, bright blue eyes, and a smile and demeanor that captured my heart and stopped me in my tracks! A lot of people dream of the future. I dream of the past—my senior year.

I remember our first date. On a Friday night, I drove us to a drive-in movie in Red Wing, Minnesota. And no, I don't remember the movie. I do remember reaching down and holding her hand. Her hand was small and soft as I gently squeezed it.

It wasn't long before we were going steady. It was October 27, 1966. Every Friday night, we'd cruise the four lanes in Lake City, then we'd drive to the Frontenac ballpark. It was lined with large trees that had huge canopies. We'd always park at the third tree. There were usually three or four other cars parking at their favorite trees.

Sandra was an honor student, and I credit her with my graduating. I couldn't spell for shit. In fact, I probably couldn't spell the word *shit*. However, it's easy to use in a sentence! I wasn't in her English class, but she tutored me in spelling and writing papers for my English class. Come to think of it, she even wrote a few papers for me.

Looking back, I believe studying *Romeo and Juliet* was a waste of my time and the taxpayers' money. I believe it still is today for some students. Some individuals are mentally gifted for that type of learning. I wasn't. My knowledge was gained by hanging on to a steering wheel and shifting gears, watching Uncle Ray or my dad dismantle engines to make repairs, and so on.

Unfortunately, you have some highly intellectual teachers who think everybody should be blessed to learn *Romeo and Juliet*. But when students receive Ds or Fs, the teachers scratch their heads with disbelief, make the students stay after class, treating them like losers. These intellectual scholars would most likely kill themselves if they had to use the empirical method to learn how to operate dangerous farm machinery. Why? Because not all humans are wired the same. When I was growing up, though, this wasn't recognized. These intellectuals I refer to are book smart and street stupid. Oh, do I have the examples.

My senior year went fast. Before I knew it, I had to decide what I would do when I graduated high school. I didn't see myself as college material. And I knew if I didn't enlist, I'd most likely get a draft notice in the mail from Uncle Sam. The government was taking most every young man available—except those who had legal exemptions or who had deserted to Canada.

Many of those drafted were sent to Vietnam as ground pounders, or foot soldiers. And 58,000 of them didn't make it home. The Vietnam War was hell, and the foot soldiers experienced the worst of it. Read about Hamburger Hill—just one of many disasters during the war. In reality, though, whether you were enlisted or drafted, the mere thought of being sent to *war* was terrifying!

From an early age, I had wanted to join the navy and become a machinist's mate, like Olaf. He had just been discharged after eight years of service. His training as a machinist's mate enabled him to land a well-paying job as a boiler operator at the University of Minnesota.

So, on March 27, 1967, I enlisted in the 120-day delay program, which allowed me to finish the school year before reporting to active duty. I was sworn into the navy before I graduated. I would leave for boot camp on July 27.

Sandra and I were in love, and we decided to commit to each other. We got engaged before I left for boot camp. Sandra had decided to enter college after graduation. Our plan was for Sandra to complete college while I was in the navy. Upon my discharge, we'd get married. It was the dream we shared together.

But we were young. We didn't realize just how painful it would be to be apart, just how much loneliness we'd experience, and just how profound of an effect the military and the separation from each other would have on our future relationship. Each goodbye, each separation, would be harder and harder, with more and more tears of sadness shed.

I sold my blue 1963 Chevrolet 409 and bought Sandra an engagement ring in early summer 1967. Nothing would separate our love for each other.

Before we knew it, we were saying goodbye, and I was off to boot camp. It was the first of many tearful separations. It set a path of loneliness and a hunger for each other's touch. To quote the Righteous Brothers from their song in 1966: "You're my soul and my heart's inspiration. You're all I've got to get me by . . . I can't make it without you." Sandra hung with me, and she was my drive to succeed.

Chapter 3

Leaving Home: Boot Camp

A Boeing 707 takes me and 149 other recruits to San Diego.

I was about to embark on a four-year journey in the United States Navy. What prepared me for this experience wasn't the last four years of senior high school. Rather, it was my last eleven years of empirical learning from my older brother, my dad, my uncle, the Fair Hills Farm, and the Rambler dealership. Thankfully, I had grown and developed in a non-structured learning environment—the street, so to say.

This set the foundation for placement in a naval vocation that would allow me to excel and succeed during the next four years. The navy did a very good job evaluating new recruits for the type of military position they'd best perform in. After a battery of tests during boot camp, their vocation selection for me was spot-on: a machinist's mate.

Dad drove me up to the Federal Building in Minneapolis on the morning of July 27, 1967. When he stopped the car in front of the building, the only word we could both verbally express was "Goodbye." He shook my hand before I opened the door to climb out. His chin trembled. We both had tears in our eyes. And then I walked away. Dad and I were close, and saying goodbye was profound. We both knew our daily lives would forever change.

At the Federal Building, I was grouped with other new recruits before we were bused to the Minneapolis–Saint Paul airport. We boarded a Boeing 707 jet aircraft. It was big and chartered only for recruits.

This was the first jet airplane I'd flown in. I'd never liked carnival rides, so I wasn't sure about this huge plane. Also, this would be my first time out of the state of Minnesota. I didn't realize it at the time, but I was about to experience a lot of firsts. And most them, as I remember, were less than desirable.

I was sitting in the aisle seat, and a stewardess was serving pop with her back to me. All of a sudden, the recruit sitting next to me in the center seat reached over and pinched the stewardess in the ass. This was an oh-shit moment!

The stewardess whirled around, pissed. Assuming I had done it from the aisle seat, she aggressively reprimanded me, yelling at me for bad behavior. As I tried explained that I didn't do it, several other recruits started laughing. Then she proceeded to scold all of us. If that had happened today, an air marshal would have put us in cuffs, and we'd be going to jail instead of boot camp.

The plane landed in San Diego around midnight. We were escorted off the plane and bused to an intake center. We disembarked the bus and lined up on the asphalt. The air was warm and humid. I remember seeing palm trees for the first time as they moved slightly in the warm breeze. That's the only pleasant thought I remember.

I also remember being greeted by a striking marine drill sergeant using verbal intimidation meant to instill the fear of God into you. You quickly understood who was in charge, and you were told to keep your mouth shut, speak when spoken to, and do exactly as you were told. After verbally abusing us for about a half hour, they figured they had our attention. We were loaded on a bus for transfer to the Naval Training Center. There, I would spend the next nine weeks in boot camp to develop the knowledge and skills needed to survive in the United States Navy.

The first night, I was assigned to the top rack of three bunk beds. I was in temporary barracks with a couple hundred recruits, all strangers. It was an atmosphere of apprehension and fear through the eyes of an eighteen-year-old.

It was about 1:30 a.m. on July 28 when all lights finally went out and no one was wandering around. When they ordered you to get in your rack, they weren't waiting for stragglers—they meant immediately.

That first night was mentally hard after the lights went out. I remember thinking, *Holy shit. What did I get myself into?* I had been away from home for three months at a time during several summers, so it wasn't as though I had never left home. But this was permanent, and reality was setting in: this wasn't going to be like my memorable summer stays with Uncle Ray.

At exactly 4:30 a.m.—or better yet, 0430—the lights came on, and you heard yelling to get up out of your rack. Everybody was thinking, *What's the problem? Why are we getting up so early?* But it wasn't a question you asked out loud. Again, you didn't speak unless spoken to, and there was no conversation between the recruits. But everyone's thoughts were the same.

You quickly figured out this would be a daily routine. Standing at attention in front of our racks, we were given instructions—forty-five minutes to shit, shower, shave, and then fall in line to march to the chow hall. From that point forward for the next nine weeks, wherever we went, we marched or ran.

After chow, we marched over to our barracks, where we met our company commander (CC). His job was to "push" fifty-six recruits through nine weeks of boot camp. He was an E-6, petty officer first class aviation boatswain's mate.

One of the first things the navy took from you was your hair. A buzz job was in order, and you didn't even have to pay for it. Our CC marched his new recruits over to the barbershop, and we waited in line for a haircut. By the way, the navy was "hurry up and wait." This was the standard my next four years. A lot of rushing somewhere just to stand in line.

Back in the 1960s, there were a lot of long-haired hippies impressed and in love with their long hair. With each swipe of the shears, their hair dropped to the floor, and the defeated looks on their faces became more pronounced.

These barbers didn't give you the kind of attention you receive at Sport Clips. If they accidentally scratched your scalp with the shears because they were in a hurry—which they were—too bad.

During the next nine weeks, the barbers kept the sides cut close but allowed the top to grow out a bit. This was Southern California in the middle of summer. A head with no hair would sunburn very quickly. To also prevent sunburn, everybody was issued a ball cap, which you were ordered to wear whenever outside, no exceptions. If they caught you outside without your cap on, it wasn't "Please put your ball cap on, recruit." Instead, they'd yell, "Hey, squirrel—put you're fucking cap on!"

In fact, if you did anything wrong in boot camp, the CC wouldn't sit you down, hold your hand, and explain your mistake with loving words. He'd yell at you for screwing up. And to make sure he had your attention, he'd give you a chit to attend a "working party" that evening, when the rest of your company was given time to write letters home.

No one at the Naval Training Center was nice to you. It was their job to be assholes and to break the recruits of all past habits, negative traits, and behaviors that weren't conducive to the navy's way of thinking and way of life. If you didn't get the message the first time, they had more ways to persuade you, taking your life from difficult to miserable.

On Sunday, Company 432 was awakened at 0530 with the loud crash of a twenty-five-gallon metal garbage can being kicked and rolled down the center isle of the barracks. It was very loud, startling, and not a pleasant way to be woken up from a sound sleep. They not only wanted your immediate attention, they wanted to scare the living shit out of you so you wouldn't forget who the hell was in charge.

Again, those who didn't demonstrate that they got the message would receive correctional lessons on the Grinder. The Grinder was an area of asphalt baked hot in the California sun. Correctional lessons were push-ups, sit-ups, jumping jacks, etc. The combination of the exercise and the hot asphalt was a deterrent and a clear message to change your behavior.

We marched to the chow hall for our morning meal. Then we took care of our housekeeping duties. Next, we were asked, "Who wants to go to church?" I remember only about half the recruits raised their hands. The other half didn't want to go to church. But the CC checked the dog tags of those who didn't raise their hands. At the Federal Building during enlistment, you were asked your religious affiliation, and your answer was stamped into your dog tags. So unless your dog tag said "Atheist," you were going to church. Everyone went to church.

My first week in boot camp, I was issued navy clothes and shoes. On each piece of clothing, I stenciled my last name and serial number—a number I'll never forget. I was issued a seabag in which I had to fit everything I owned when traveling between assignments or traveling on leave. We were taught how to fold each piece of clothing when packing the seabag so we could unpack and still wear our uniform to an inspection, if required.

Our CC presented our company flag with the number 432. This flag was flown when we marched to and from our barracks. All recruits learned to march with a military-issued nine-pound rifle—the barrel filled with lead. The company would practice marching every morning on the Grinder to prepare for week 9-2, our boot camp graduation ceremony. (Time at boot camp was expressed by week and day. For example, week 1-2 meant week one, day two; week 3-3 was week 3, day 3.)

Week one included navy assessment screening to determine your best skill set. The results would then decide your duty placement aboard ship, so you could best serve the ship's mission. If you had a high aptitude in the mechanical field, which I did, you would most likely be assigned to the engineering division as a fireman apprentice (E-2).

On week 1-2, we marched to the PX (post exchange, or naval store) to purchase necessities such as writing paper, soap, razors, and so on. Then we boxed up everything we brought from home, including our clothes, and it was all mailed back. We weren't allowed to keep anything from home. We could keep only the items that were issued or that we purchased at the PX. Everything you owned was now stored in a small metal cabinet assigned next to your bunk.

Each recruit had to stand a two-hour watch at night. This meant you received about six hours of sleep every day. And there was no "shut-eye" during the day. The CC left you with very little downtime.

Inspections were conducted daily, and the barracks had to be spotless. We cleaned the grout in the tile wall with a toothbrush to ensure the grout was white. Needless to say, there was no dirt in the cracks.

You washed your clothes by hand outside on a large concrete table. After rinsing, you'd hang each piece very neatly and well organized on a clothesline to dry overnight. You were also taught how to fold and stow your clothes in your metal cabinet along with your bath towels. The CC did not appreciate discrepancies in how you folded your clothes. Your bunk was made with the utmost care as well, ensuring that no discrepancies would be noted during morning inspection. Your locker was inspected daily for proper placement.

Each company was in competition for points. The company with the most points was rewarded with a patch or an additional flag to display on or with their company flag. Each company took pride in the number of patches and flags displayed.

And if you didn't have many—or any—your CC would be like a cub bear with a sore dick—he wouldn't be happy. He'd become Mr. Asshole. Each CC was graded on how well he pushed his company from week 1-1 through graduation. Anyone bringing the company down would be in the CC's crosshairs.

Thinking back to my days with high school sports, I

remember how the whole team suffered when one athlete screwed up. Not in the navy. The one who screwed up received all the attention—called a "marching party." Not fun.

On 1-3, our company was in formation near the barracks, and our CC ordered all recruits to fall out and gather around him. I remember his voice slightly cracking as he began telling us about a major accident on the flight deck of the USS *Forrestal* on July 29, 1967, stationed off the coast of Vietnam. The accident killed 134 sailors and injured 161. The USS *Forrestal* was our CC's last duty station, where he served as an aviation boatswain's mate. He personally knew many of those killed and injured.

A mistake turns into a disaster on the USS Forrestal.

This USS *Forrestal* disaster directly involved Lt. Cmdr. John McCain, who is now an Arizona senator. Formerly, he was a naval pilot who rose to the rank of captain before retiring from the United States Navy. On the day of the accident, McCain was seated in his A-4 jet aircraft, waiting to taxi toward the catapult. He was preparing for launch on a bombing mission over Vietnam.

Without warning, a Zuni missile accidently launched from the wing of another jet plane, striking McCain's belly fuel tank. Fuel from McCain's A-4 belly tank spilled out and caught fire. The fire then spread to planes on the flight deck and detonated a thousand-pound bomb, which killed many of the initial firefighters and further spread the fire. Then a chain reaction of explosions blew additional holes in the flight deck. Now, half of the aircraft carrier was on fire. Many pilots were trapped in their planes as the fire spread.

It took a full day before the fire was contained. It was a massive heroic undertaking by the sailors to extinguish the fire and save their ship. The USS *Forrestal* was severely damaged and had to return to port for extensive repairs.

Thankfully, Lt. Cmdr. McCain escaped from his plane and made it to sick bay for treatment of his shrapnel wounds and burns. He's spoken of the horrible scene in sick bay of men burned beyond saving and grasping the last moments of life. Unable to keep composure, he left sick bay. (I have great respect for Senator McCain, his father, and grandfather. There will be more on the McCains later.)

When I first heard about this horrific accident, I understood the loss of life and why our company commander was grieving. But I didn't fully grasp how this accident was just one example of the continuous danger that surrounds sailors aboard an aircraft carrier and other naval ships deployed for combat operations off the coast of Vietnam.

When I look back now, though, I realize just how quickly controlled danger can turn into a disaster causing injury, death, and destruction aboard a warship. Somehow, I survived. Either I was damn lucky or faith played a part. I believe it's the latter. I was in numerous situations that could have turned disastrous had it not been for a godsend or a miracle.

Week 1-1, Company 432 was informed we'd graduate on 9-2 and granted military leave on 9-5. That is, unless the company required an additional week of training due to a lack of skills.

Week 2 included shots. Yes, plural. Our company marched to the infirmary, where we were told to strip to our waist and fall in line. There were two corpsmen, one on each side of the line. As you stepped in between them, they pushed an air gun tight to each arm and pulled the trigger. That was another oh-shit moment and another first—but not the last. Every time I turned around, I was getting a shot for something, especially before my deployments to Vietnam.

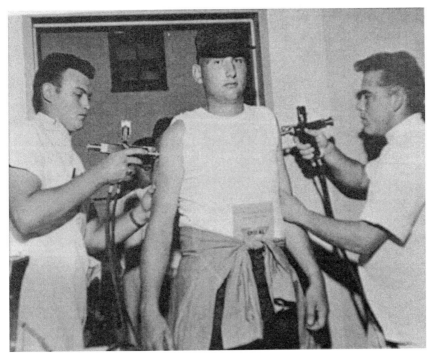

A sailor on boot camp vaccination day—hang on!

Week 2 also included a battery of tests to determine your skills aptitude and your job placement after boot camp.

Week 2-1, I was assigned the clothesline watch from 2330 to 0130. I walked a two-hour security patrol around the clothesline with a nine-pound rife filled with lead on my shoulder. Whenever passenger jets passed overhead, I'd look up, wishing I were on it. I marched around the clothesline, alert and following the orders provided. If you were caught neglecting your watch for any reason, there would be hell to pay.

At the time, I looked at this as a worthless event and navy bullshit. However, once aboard the ship, I understood how important it was for everyone to maintain the highest level of alertness and to always follow directions. You might think you've been tasked with a less-than-critical responsibility, but you could still jeopardize the ship's mission and cause life-threatening risk if you didn't maintain attention to detail.

The navy saw this as mental conditioning. The navy instilled in you early on that deviation from your duty was completely unacceptable and that the severity of neglecting your duty or orders could send a sailor to "captain's mast." Captain's mast was military justice authorized by Article 15 of the Uniform Code of Military Justice. It was nonjudicial punishment and allowed the captain to administratively discipline the sailors without a court-martial. The navy isn't a democracy. You follow the chain of command and you do as you're told, with no questions asked. Period.

Clothesline detail

Mail call was now a daily event, and it always felt like Christmas! However, it continued only if Company 432, as a unit, was performing. If not, mail call was one of many tools the CC would use as leverage to ensure his company performed to his expectation.

Mail was our only contact with the outside world. We were isolated. Boot camp didn't allow TV, newspapers, and so on. It wasn't until week 5-1 that we were finally allowed one phone call home. I loved my parents, but I called Sandra with an earnest desire to hear her voice. The CC also provided a radio after week 5-1. A senior recruit got to control it. If Company 432 was passing inspections, marching in step, and the such, he'd get to turn on the radio for a short period before "Taps" and lights-out in the evening.

Week 2-3, I completed the "dream sheet" paperwork, requesting transfer to Florida after boot camp. I hoped to serve in the same location as my brother Paul. He was land based. In fact, to his credit, he never served on a ship or at sea during his four-year tour in the navy.

I performed well on the mechanical section of the navy assessment screening, so, I assumed the navy would most likely assign me to an engineering division. And all engineering divisions in the navy were ship based. Still, I had my fingers crossed for Florida.

Week 3-1, Company 432 marched in review and won the infantry flag as a platoon. This allowed our company to go ahead of the line for chow that week.

Eating in the chow hall was very organized. Each company had a chow runner, who had to double-time (run) to the chow hall and request a time to eat. Upon receiving a time, the chow runner would then double-time back to the company and report to the senior recruit.

Arriving at the chow hall at your specified time, you would fall out, line up, grab a metal tray, and proceed through the chow line. There was no hanging loose and socializing. You ate whatever you took, and ten to fifteen minutes later, you were marching back to your barracks. Those who were overweight usually lost weight. Me, I gained ten pounds in boot camp—up to 165 pounds.

Week 4-1, I had galley assignment, starting every morning at 0230. I still also had to stand a two-hour watch at night, so I was down to about two and a half hours of sleep. This made for a long day. On galley assignment, my job was to prepare the bread and serve the recruits coming through the chow line.

Week 5-1, we were informed that we were about to experience the gas chamber drill. And then on 5-2, Company 432 was marched into the tear-gas chamber, and each recruit was given a gas mask to put on. They then released tear gas into the chamber. After several minutes, tear gas filled the chamber as we continued to sit idle. One by one, we were instructed to stand, take off our gas mask, count to ten, then proceed outside. By the time you got to five, though, you were coughing and choking. Even when we got outside, everybody's eyes were watering and we continued to cough.

Gas chamber

Week 6-1 through 6-2, our company received instruction and training with M1 rifles at the shooting range. I scored a 98.

Rifle training

Week 6-3 through 6-5, our company received firefighting training. We learned about the three classes of fire (A, B, and C) and how to extinguish each of them. We also learned about the types of fire hoses, nozzles, chemicals, and so on. Fire is one of the biggest threats aboard a ship. And if a fire breaks out, everyone is expected to know how to combat it.

Week 7-1, I stood 4050 watch at the brig, or jail for sailors. It was a correctional unit in the navy. If our civilian jails operated like naval brigs, you'd have fewer people in jail. The brig was tough—I mean *tough*! The prisoner would wear a red sailor hat and was considered a disgrace. I remember 4050 guards bringing a prisoner through the chow line, and the recruits eating were not to look up and observe. The guards did not verbally talk to prisoners. The only communication and direction was given through whistles. I also witnessed this when I stood a watch at the 4050 brig. It was a strong reminder to stay out of trouble.

Throughout boot camp, we'd have three to four hours every day of classroom studies to learn how to properly live within the navy, its rules, regulation, chain of command, and necessary military requirements. Week 8-1 was the final test pertaining to naval life. If you didn't pass, you were dropped back a week for further instruction.

Week 9-2, I learned that airfare home from San Diego would be sixty-seven dollars, whereas I could fly standby for forty-seven. That twenty-buck savings was a lot of money in 1967. I decided to look into flying standby.

The government gave you a free flight *to* boot camp; however, you had to pay for airfare home *from* boot camp. I think that first flight was the only free thing I received from the military. Even the military clothes we were issued during our first week of boot camp came out of our pay, which was less than $100 per month.

The CC informed our company that we would graduate during the week of 9-3. Good news! But then on 9-2, I wrote Sandra with bad news: "I've received orders to report to the USS *Hancock* (CVA-19) on November 13 at 2400 hours." Sandra and I were counting on a transfer to Florida so I could be stationed with Paul and so Sandra and I could be closer.

Week 9-3, I talked with the base chaplain about wanting to be stationed in Florida, hoping he could help. I explained that Paul was stationed there too. The chaplain told me I couldn't go with Paul because he was shore duty. In reality, the navy needed every able body coming out of boot camp to man the ships engaged in the Vietnam War.

Boot camp was difficult and challenging, but what we learned there was necessary to our survival once we reported to the fleet. The day we left boot camp, I remember lining up as the CC walked past his recruits, shaking our hands and wishing each of us the best. As strict as he was, he showed he cared and had heart. His heavy hand was in our best interest, and I'm grateful to him.

Arriving home from boot camp on military leave prior to reporting to the USS *Hancock*, I met Sandra and my dad at the airport—big smiles, hugs, and kisses. Sandra and I spent as much time together as possible. However, she was in college at the University of Wisconsin–Stout, which meant I did a lot of commuting from Lake City to Wisconsin.

While home on military leave, Sandra and I celebrated a special moment on October 28, 1967. It was one year exactly from when I asked her to go steady with me. Most likely it had been a chilly autumn night, and we had been parked at our favorite tree at the Frontenac ballpark.

My leave went fast. Sandra and I said goodbye to each other two days before I was to report to the USS *Hancock*. But on my last day at home, I borrowed Dad's car and drove over to Wisconsin to see Sandra one more time before I left. It was about five o'clock, and she was surprised to see me. We sat in the car until midnight, talking about our future and sharing each other's company.

Saying goodbye was getting harder each time we separated. I walked her to her dorm, the tears flowing down our cheeks. We kissed goodbye, and I turned and walked away. This was one of many painful separations.

Chapter 4
Reporting aboard the USS *Hancock*

USS Hancock, *USS* Midway, *and USS* Ranger *at Hunters Point Naval Shipyard*

November 13, 1967

D ad drove me to the airport, and I caught an early flight to San Francisco. I then took a cab to Hunters Point Naval Shipyard, where the USS *Hancock* was in dry dock. It was my first experience seeing a huge aircraft carrier sitting in this big concrete bathtub.

I walked up the enlisted gangplank to board the ship and was met by a chief petty officer. He looked through my orders and made a call to M Division for an escort. The good news, I got my wish—I was an E-2 fireman apprentice striking for the machinist's mate rate and assigned to the aft engine room. I was following in my brother's footsteps.

The bad news, an E-2 fireman apprentice was the lowest rung of the ladder. When you know nothing about the engine room, you're assigned the dirtiest, most miserable tasks, such as cleaning the bilges, grinding and chipping lead paint in the voids of the ship, insulating steam lines with asbestos, and more. Understand, these tasks must be completed. Most petty officers and officers overseeing these tasks understood the misery involved and therefore treated their subordinates with respect. However, there were a few who treated you like a grunt, making life aboard the ship even more painful, mentally and physically.

After entering the aft engine room via a steep ladder, my first experience was looking up and seeing that a number of metal decks had been removed via a cutting torch. I could see up to the hanger bay above. The thick metal decks had been cut out so the yardbirds—the contract workers who repaired and upgraded the ship while in port—could remove and repair the eight-foot-diameter bow gear from the Number 2 main engine. Once the bow gear was eventually lowered back down to the engine room, it took about a month of the yardbirds welding twenty-four hours per day to refit and secure all the decks—including the two-and-a-half-inch-thick hanger bay deck.

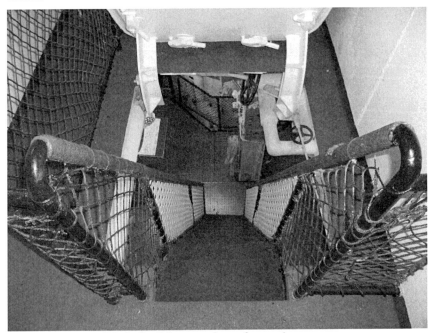

Ship's ladder to the aft engine room

The aft engine room was an engineering compartment situated below the waterline. It contained two main engines powered by high-pressure steam and the necessary auxiliary support equipment to turn two screws propelling the ship. Each main engine included both a high-pressure and a low-pressure turbine, each producing 37,500 horsepower. The two main engines in the forward engine room did the same. The four main engines had a combined horsepower of 150,000.

The USS *Hancock* could reach a speed of thirty-three knots, or thirty-eight miles, per hour. I still remember the sound of the high-pressure steam whistling through the steam lines, the high-pitch whine of the turbines, and—most of all—

the smooth vibration of the main engines and the deck plates under your feet at flank speed.

Later, when I became the engine room's top watch and the bridge ordered flank speed, hanging on to 75,000 horsepower was an adrenalin rush! It reminded me of powering the diesel tractor up a long, winding hill as a young boy. (Except I saw no black smoke.)

The four turbine engines were powered by eight boilers producing 600 pounds per square inch (psi) of steam at 850-degree superheat. Each main engine was connected via reduction gearing to a thirteen-inch-diameter steel shaft. The shaft extended from the reduction gear through the bowels of the ship, to the ship's stern. The shaft then extended through the ship's hull via a packing gland to the outside of the ship, where four screws sixteen feet in diameter and 16,000 pounds each were attached.

For this old WWII ship, the control and operation of the forward and aft engine rooms was totally manual. There were no electronics, computers, or automation systems. Starting the main engines wasn't as easy as turning a key or programing a computer. Readying the engine room for commands from the bridge was called lighting off. The light-off process involved a sequence of events that took the engine room top watch approximately four to six hours to complete. You had to configure numerous systems; coordinate with main control and Number 3 and Number 4 boiler rooms; start the booster and condensate pumps, the lube oil pumps, and the steam-driven circ-pumps; develop and maintain a twenty-eight-inch vacuum on both engines; open and close valves; and more.

And that was just the light-off process. There were also a multitude of complex machinery and system sequences for the process of getting underway. There were speed changes, emergencies, and causality control. A depth of knowledge was needed to configure and manage the engine room's extremely volatile systems. And it was all imperative to the mission of a warship.

As an eighteen-year-old, I understood the operation and mechanics of an internal combustion engine used to power an automobile. But my first experience entering the engine room and seeing the maze of piping, valves, pumps, tanks, heat exchangers, numerous systems, and two steam-turbine-driven engines was overwhelming, to say the least. Operating the engine room and managing the constant danger of its volatile systems required a highly trained and mentally disciplined petty officer.

Another first experience that day was walking into the berthing compartment, or the sleeping quarters. The M Division berthing compartment contained seventy racks stacked three, sometimes four, high with an isle between the racks about three feet wide. There were seventy small metal steaming lockers—one for each sailor to stow everything he owned while at sea.

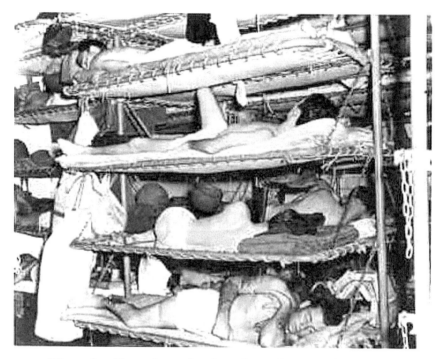

Note the dirty-laundry bag hanging on the racks.

The sailor with the highest rank had first choice of bunk, while the non-rate ended up with the bottom bunk in the worst location in the berthing compartment. Sleeping three sailors deep wasn't easy. You had to make sure the rope securing your bunk's canvas to the metal frame was tight. If not, the middle of canvas, where your ass lay, would sag into the sleeping area of the sailor below, making that sailor very unhappy.

The berthing compartment was cleaned daily by non-rates overseen by a petty officer. Each sailor was responsible for changing his fart sack—the mattress cover. A laundry bag hung on the racks for your dirty clothes, which were sent to the laundry several times a week. Your name was stenciled on your clothes so the non-rates could sort and return them to your rack.

When your clothes came back from the ship's laundry, they didn't look or smell as if your mother just washed them. Your shirt and pants were severely winkled, and they faded more with each wash. When you put on your clothes, you looked a little disheveled.

I was a young sailor who had just graduated high school five months prior, and my life experiences were changing by the hour. I was forced to change from a carefree teenager into a young man in the military, which demands your mistake-free attention.

Boot camp gave me the basics of naval life. But within twelve hours of boarding that aircraft carrier sitting in dry dock, I was introduced to M Division, the aft engine room, the berthing compartment with seventy other sailors (whom you don't know), new directives, and verbal harassment (we'd call it abuse nowadays). It was mentally challenging. There was no turning back!

Thanksgiving 1967

After I reported to the ship, Sandra and I traded numerous letters and several three-minute phone calls. (And long-distance calls were expensive.) Our loneliness for each other grew, as did our concern about my deployment to Vietnam. So we decided to get married and be together before the ship would leave for Vietnam in July. She told both our parents when she was home from college on Thanksgiving break.

I received a letter from Sandra's mom, Marion, saying, "Don't waste any precious time you can spend together when you're young—you'll never regret it." *She was so right!* Most parents would have discouraged their children from getting married in this situation. However, Sandra's mom and dad had been in a similar situation during World War II.

My mom and dad were also on board with our marriage. Dad accompanied Sandra to the courthouse and signed for the marriage license. The government said eighteen years of age wasn't old enough to get married without my parents' written consent. Funny—the government didn't require my parents' signature when I joined the military at age eighteen. Nor did the government ask for your parents' signature when they drafted you. It was bullshit.

Sandra would complete her first semester of college on January 3, 1968. She started to plan our wedding, and I planned to put in a chit, or request, for leave for the middle of January so I could fly home to get married.

November 29–30, 1967

An emotional Robert McNamara announced his resignation as defense secretary during a November 29 press briefing. Behind closed doors, he had been regularly expressing doubts over Johnson's war strategy.

The next day, Senator Eugene McCarthy from Minnesota announced he'd register as a candidate for president, opposing Johnson. McCarthy stated, "The entire history of this war in Vietnam has been one of continued error and misjudgment." History has proven his statement—dead on. By the end of December 1967, the United States troop level reached 463,000, with 16,000 deaths.

December 5, 1967

On December 5, I put in a chit, requesting leave to be married in January. Mr. V., the M Division officer, told me I was too young to get married. He denied my request for leave. That was a gut shot. I was supposedly too young to get married, but not too young to go to war as one of those "flowering youth" Johnson so righteously spoke of in 1965.

The words in a song sung by Barry McGuire in 1966 say it all: "You're old enough to kill but not for votin'."

Mr. V. was a chief warrant officer and a real asshole. My contempt for him is profound. So, from this point forward, I'll refer to him as Mr. Schmuck.

Mr. Schmuck never showed concern for those reporting to him. Rather, he caused much anguish among the enlisted ranks. He started his naval service in boot camp as an E-1, the lowest rank in the military. He understood what it was like to be a non-rate in the US Navy—he lived it. So, to treat his subordinates with such disdain and arrogance was wrong.

Here's an example of the anguish and toil Mr. Schmuck imposed on his men: at sea, when the outside air temperatures rose due to tropical climates, temperatures aboard the ship would as well. In those cases, the captain of the ship would set tropical working hours meant to reduce nonvital workload.

Despite the tropical working hours, Mr. Schmuck would call for M Division to muster in the engine rooms and "turn to," which means work. The engine room was one of the hottest areas on the ship. As a non-rated sailor, I would report to wire-brush the deck plates or polish the brass in 120-degree heat. But the deck plates weren't dirty, and the brass wasn't dull. I remember the first-class petty officer in charge of the aft engine room shaking his head in disgust. His nonverbal expression displayed his true feelings for his men—he cared! However, he had to follow the orders given by a senior officer.

These tasks did nothing to support the ship's mission. It was merely Mr. Schmuck piling onto the misery the enlisted personnel experienced. It only added to the lack of morale within the ranks of M division.

Despite Mr. Schmuck denying my request for leave, Sandra and I were still determined to get married. Our minds were set. For a while, we talked about her flying out to California to get married if I couldn't get leave. But after mire discussion, we decided I'd give it one more try to get leave in a few weeks. Maybe we could manage to get married in February.

Mid-December 1967

I was assigned to the Number 3 shaft alley, where Dave, a third-class petty officer from Eugene, Oregon, was my supervisor. He was highly respected for his knowledge of the engine room. Not to mention he stood about six foot two with a solid body shaped like a concrete wedge.

We became close friends, and he would become my mentor for the next six months. He was a straight-arrow individual—didn't swear, didn't drink, didn't smoke, didn't use drugs, and didn't cheat on his wife overseas. Throughout high school, I never drank, smoked, used drugs, or got in trouble with the law. So hanging around Dave kept the peer pressure off my back. Nobody screwed with him. He had the ability to deflect verbal abuse from other sailors, which left me smiling many times. And nobody challenged him physically.

I'm thankful I had a friend such as Dave right from the start because I quickly learned that naval life was hard to navigate on your own. What I'm about to write isn't meant to cast a negative shadow on my shipmates. Rather, it's to show the pressure naive young sailors encountered once aboard the ship. Only eighteen years of age, most young men came aboard with a moral code of self-respect, only to fall victim to peer pressure and the lust of adulthood. You'd take a lot of verbal abuse if you didn't follow the risqué life of the seasoned shipmates.

Aboard the ship, these young sailors struggled with the mental and physical pressure of long work hours and terrible working conditions. For a machinist's mate, the engine and boiler rooms were hot, the hours were long, and life turned into a daily grind for months at a time.

A sailor's free time away from the ship was called liberty— a fitting term in many ways. And for most sailors, going on liberty meant the low-hanging fruit of smoking, drinking, drugs, prostitutes, and barroom fights. After thirty days of combat operations at sea, many young sailors wanted only a "good time" on the town with no worries about tomorrow. The harsh conditions of the war pushed many sailors over the edge and onto the path of wrongdoing. Not an excuse—just an observation.

On top of it all, those sailors who made unsavory decisions placed a lot of peer pressure on those who perhaps didn't want to follow the same lifestyle. An eighteen-year-old joining the military back in the 1960s was instantly introduced to the swamp of ill repute. Without a strong constitution, he would succumb to it and become one of them.

As I look back, I believe the unsavory sailors pressured the others by creating an "everyone does it" environment, justifying the behavior in their minds. Because if even one or two sailors wouldn't lower their dignity and bow to these unsavory transgressions, then the others would internally feel shame.

Then again, some sailors were just plain pigs with no guilt or shame. They didn't care what other sailors thought or did. They wore their actions as a badge of honor. It was all a big laugh.

Of all the unsavory behaviors, many sailors thought they could hide the truth and get away with prostituted sex. And yes, some of those were married. Often after the ship left a foreign port, there would be two lines to sick bay: one line for those who had the usual ailments and another (extending up to the hanger bay) for those with venereal disease (VD).

One VD was called non-specific urethritis (NSU). If a sailor had unprotected sex with an infected woman in a foreign port, his lower unit would start dripping about a week or so later. He'd then report to sick bay and receive medicine to treat the VD and curb the dripping. The problem was that NSU could reoccur in the future. Many sailors experienced a reoccurrence when living back home in the States with their wives. Now the sailor had to explain to his wife why his lower unit was dripping—more lies. Also, if not careful, he could infect his wife.

The combination of peer pressure and harsh conditions made many sailors lose their way—even those who tried so hard to stay on the right path. In my time in the navy, I witness a forward engine room machinist's mate fall from his path. During his first deployment, he resisted the adultery that went along with the bar life in foreign ports. But then one night, in the Philippine Islands, he succumbed to the peer pressure, alcohol, and bar environment of young prostitutes. He cheated on his wife.

I remember his demeanor the next morning, back on the ship, as he realized what he had done. He was mentally shaken. I can still see his face as he broke down in tears. He had crossed the line and couldn't go back. He realized he had broken the commandment "Thou shall not commit adultery." In his tears of sorrow, he questioned how he would explain his betrayal to his newly married wife.

Like that sailor, I had to make choices during my time in the navy. I'm thankful I had a steady guide right from the start in Dave. Dave was discharged from the navy in July 1968, a week before my first deployment to Vietnam. But for the six months I knew him, he laid the groundwork for my future growth as a machinist's mate. More importantly, he showed me how to carry myself with respect and dignity over the next three and a half years.

What I learned from Dave wasn't taught in any naval manuals. I've had many godsends throughout my years, and meeting Dave at that time of my life was indeed a godsend.

December 17, 1968

Dear Sandra,

The first-class petty officer in charge of the aft engine room informed his crew the ship is leaving the dry dock on December 17 and a two-week shakedown cruise is scheduled for April 16. The USS Enterprise is deploying to Vietnam in January, which means there will be lots of apartments open in Alameda. There's a good possibility of finding an apartment if we can get married in February and you fly back with me. The apartment building where Dave and his wife are staying is a thirty-minute walk to the Alameda naval air base. I'll catch a liberty launch to and from the air base over to Hunters Point Shipyard.

I've gained another two pounds, and I'm up to 167 pounds. The food at the base galley has been very good, and I'm getting plenty to eat. The galley on the ship is closed during the yard period and is schedule to reopen on January 27. I'm standing "cold iron watch" as a messenger and studying to take my E-3 fireman's test in February.

December 19, 1967

Still determined to get married, I requested two days' leave to make a four-day weekend, February 2 through February 5. This would allow just enough time to fly home to get married. Dave was in tight with the aft engine room's first class and lobbied hard on my behalf.

My chit was sent on to M Division Office. Amazingly, Mr. Schmuck signed off on it. I had four days to fly home and get married. The wedding date was set for Saturday, February 3. I had to report back to the ship no later than 0700 on Tuesday, February 6.

January 1968

Sandra and I were both excited. February 3 was approaching fast, and we were looking forward to marriage and being together.

After Sandra finished the last week of college, she and my dad went to the county courthouse to apply for our marriage license. She bought her dress and veil and decided on the invitations, flowers, cake, and the material for her attendants' dresses. She picked out my ring and met with the minister as well.

On January 12, I sent Sandra my measurements for my tux, and she picked up her veil. She said it was beautiful. On January 15, Dad and Sandra picked up the marriage license. And on January 27, she picked up her dress.

In just over a month, Sandra had pulled together a church wedding with five attendants and five groomsmen—a task that would take most a year to do.

While Sandra planned the wedding back home, I looked into getting us an apartment. Dave invited me over to his apartment, and his wife, Darlene, fixed supper for us both. Dave then introduced me to his apartment manager, so I could discuss apartment availability and the monthly rental rate of eighty-three dollars per month.

I knew Sandra and I would need every penny we could earn and save. I decided to loan all my money—thirty dollars—to sailors in M Division going on liberty. The going lending rate was five dollars for seven dollars or ten dollars for fourteen dollars. Providing everybody paid me back, I stood to make twenty dollars on my thirty.

I also "stood by," or covered duties for sailors wanting extra liberty. I got paid fourteen dollars for a two-day weekend. So in one month, the extra income equaled my net monthly income I received from the navy.

That month, I also had my first direct experience with what I call the hidden enemies aboard ship. I had temporary assigned duty (TAD) with a lagging crew insulating the ceiling, breaching, and bulkheads of the Number 3 and 4 firerooms. I was in direct contact with asbestos materials and a milky adhesive liquid containing polychlorinated biphenyl (PCB), which contained dioxin. Dioxin is part of the herbicide Agent Orange, which was used extensively in-country to destroy enemy cover.

We dipped cheesecloth in this milky liquid and formed it over the asbestos lagging to retain heat. My hands and arms were covered with adhesive, and my hands became raw due to the long hours working with these materials.

Asbestos and PCBs were not the only invisible enemies my shipmates and I were exposed to during our time in the navy. We were exposed to fine particles of lead dust when grinding and chipping lead paint, harmful chemicals when degreasing machinery parts, carbon when breathing burned black oil, and more. Though located throughout the ship, these chemicals and fumes were especially concentrated in engineering divisions aboard the older WWII military ships.

Our government was aware of the potential danger to sailors' future health, but our leaders chose to turn a blind eye in order to serve America's military mission. And so these chemicals caused long-term injury and death to thousands of sailors.

Today, the Department of Veterans Affairs (VA) continues to turn a blind eye to the health problems caused by the invisible enemies and shipboard hazards of pre-1970 military ships. The VA disability guidelines consist of thousands of pages of regulations written by lawyers and medical staff. It's almost impossible for a veteran without a legal or medical background to file a successful disability claim. And many organizations filing disability claims for the veterans through power of attorney are politically and financially connected with the VA. As I call it, they're "in the tank."

Current congressional law requires the VA to assist veterans with their disability claims, but it doesn't happen. It's just the opposite: the VA imposes every roadblock possible to ensure claims are denied. I've been there—as you'll find out later in the book.

January 23, 1968

The USS *Pueblo* (AGER-2), a navy intelligence ship engaged in routine surveillance off the North Korean coast, was attacked and captured by North Korean patrol boats. The North Koreans opened fire, wounding the ship's commander and two other sailors. The *Pueblo* was boarded and taken to Wonsan, North Korea, where it remains today as a symbol of dominance over the United States. Imprisoned for eleven months, the eighty-three sailors aboard the *Pueblo* were charged with spying within North Korea's twelve-mile territorial limit. The United States, however, stated the *Pueblo* was sixteen miles from shore, in international water.

Earlier in the book, I wrote about President Johnson complaining about North Vietnam harassing the USS *Maddox* in the Gulf of Tonkin. Calling it "open aggression on the high seas," Johnson used that incident to escalate the Vietnam War. Well, if capturing a United States Navy vessel and imprisoning its sailors isn't considered "open aggression on the high seas" and an "act of war," what is?

President Johnson should have immediately, without warning, ended the Korean Armistice Agreement and bombed the shit out of the North Korean leadership using tactical nukes. He should have bombed them until they said uncle and surrendered, as Truman did to Japan in WWII. But by not responding to this incident, Johnson showed North Korea, China, Russia, and North Vietnam that he was weak. Period!

These are the tough decisions a commander in chief needs to make. If Johnson and his administration had the proper foresight and grit, the United States wouldn't have the problems with North Korea and its thirty-six-year-old demented leader that we have today. The problem with North and South Korea would have been over fifty years ago.

It is true that we might have lost our prisoners in the bombing. However, the United States was losing one thousand soldiers per month in Vietnam, which the White House seemed to consider acceptable—my words. Keep in mind that our soldiers and sailors knowingly put their lives on the line when they sign their names to enter the military. It's a blank personal check to America.

It was definitely something I understood—especially in the days leading up to our wedding. The more I learned about the engine room and the ship, the more I realized how a mistake could turn into a life-ending disaster, as happened on the USS *Forrestal* in July 1967. During the month of January, my thoughts would shift to Marian's words, convincing me that Sandra and I were making the right decision to be together before I deployed to Vietnam.

Chapter 5

February 3, 1968: Married

Sandra and her dad

February 1–2, 1968

On the evening of February 1, I finished insulating the Number 3 boiler room forced-draft blower and ductwork. I then cleaned up and proceeded to the enlisted gangplank, where the officer of the deck signed my liberty papers at 0001 (one minute after midnight) on February 2. I grabbed a cab to the San Francisco airport with another machinist's mate flying out that night, splitting the fare. Flying standby, I caught the red-eye flight to

Minneapolis, arriving home early in the morning.

Sandra and I hadn't seen each other for three months. Just to hear her voice and see her face again was a joy unexplainable except to those who have experienced military separation. Time alone was limited. I caught a couple hours' sleep, then we were off for four days packed with ongoing events.

First, Sandra and I met with Pastor Goede for consultation. We met with him again that afternoon so I could be baptized. Sandra's brother, Mike, was my godfather. I had grown up Christian but had never been baptized. Sandra strongly encouraged my reaffirmation to Christianity. We didn't dwell on how my Vietnam deployment impacted that decision, but it was always in the back of our minds. I'll always remember standing before Pastor Goede that afternoon. He would pass away September 2, 2016, at age ninety-five.

That evening, we held the wedding rehearsal. It was great to catch up with several of my friends from Farmington, who were in the wedding. I hadn't seen them since I left for boot camp.

In fact, the wedding would turn out to be the last time I'd see Marvin, a groomsman and best friend through grade school and senior high. Sandra and I would attend his funeral in December 1971. Marv was one of the 58,000 military personnel who died in the Vietnam War—a war our government gave up on in 1975. Strong words, but true.

I can attest that Johnson was correct when he said, "How their mothers weep and how their families sorrow." When I left the church after Marv's funeral, I saw his mom and dad grief stricken. It hurt. Marv's dad was totally broken with sorrow.

February 3, 1968

After a very busy morning and afternoon, I suddenly found myself standing alone in the church office, waiting to enter the sanctuary to begin the ceremony. I remember thinking to myself, *If the clock could just stop for a few seconds* . . . Things were occurring so fast that there was little time to savor the moments.

I entered the sanctuary and stood in front of Pastor Goede. Sandra and her dad started their walk down the main aisle from the back of the church. I remember looking out—the church was filled with family, relatives, and friends. Sandra looked beautiful in her white wedding dress with a long veil. Arm in arm with her dad, she had that glow I saw on the first day we met at the entrance of the high school, a year and a half earlier. She was beautiful. Another moment in time I'll never forget.

Mike lent us his 1967 Fairlane to use for the wedding and honeymoon. As we exited the church, we discovered it was decorated with well-wishes. This was a sweet ride—a hot rod of a car polished to a deep shine and with strings of tin cans tied to the back bumper. We were very appreciative.

After the reception in the church basement, we drove to Rochester late that evening for our honeymoon. Again, the time passed quickly. Soon our six-hour honeymoon was over.

February 4–5, 1968

We packed up Sunday morning and drove back to Mom and Dad's resort in Lake City to open gifts. That afternoon, Dad gave us a ride to the Minneapolis airport, and we flew to San Francisco.

My cousin Marie met us at the airport and drove us to Alameda, where I had money down on a one-room apartment in Dave's building. Marie and her husband, Floyd, were very good to us. They'd invite us over for dinner and paid us to watch their house when they were out of town. Floyd was a doctor and specialized in urology. They owned a beautiful home with a large swimming pool and patio overlooking the skyline in Oakland.

I introduced Sandra to Dave and Darlene the next evening. Dave and I arranged to carpool in the morning to the Alameda naval air base, where we'd catch a liberty launch to Hunters Point Naval Shipyard.

February 6, 1968

I walked up the gangplank at 0600, and the officer of the deck signed my military leave papers, acknowledging that I had returned to the ship. At 0700, I mustered in the aft engine room for duty.

I looked back at the whirlwind four days of my leave. Sandra had orchestrated a memorable and unforgettable wedding in a very short period of time with very little money. And I now had a new responsibility as a husband. I felt the additional weight to succeed for Sandra and our future.

I'd turn nineteen in twelve days.

February 1968

Now married and living together, Sandra and I were in love and very happy, but life was hard. As an E-2 enlisted sailor, my work was difficult. Learning the operation, maintenance, and repair of the engine room was a must if I wanted to advance in rank. For the next several months, I was part of a team preparing the aft engine room for sea trials and underway training. The hours were long, and the days were even longer.

I didn't have a car, and some days I was unable to carpool. On those occasions, I'd get up at 0430 and walk to the

Alameda air base to catch the liberty launch at 0530. I always allowed myself extra time to ensure I wouldn't be late, as being late for muster meant being written up and subject to disciplinary actions.

I'd muster in the aft engine room at 0700 and work until 1530. I'd then catch a liberty launch at 1630 back to Alameda and walk back to the apartment, arriving at about 1800. Sometimes I was required to work late in the engine room, which meant getting home even later. It was a dog's life.

As an E-2, I ended up with the dirtiest work in the engine room. Sandra would fill the bathtub with hot water once I got home so I could relax and cleanup, which included washing off the asbestos I had been exposed to that day. My clothes exposed Sandra to asbestos too, as she did my laundry when I was not living on the ship.

Sandra would have supper ready after my bath, and we'd eat and talk about the day's activities and our future. Then we'd retire to bed at about 2100. I was so damn tired that as a newly married young male, I couldn't even "put a penny in the jar," so to say. But we were together, and those few hours we shared would become highly treasured memories during my long deployments. As Dave provided me principled and professional guidance, Sandra provided me unconditional strength to endure and succeed in a very depressing and demanding environment.

The ship was on three-section duty, which meant I stood duty every third day. I couldn't leave the ship on my duty days, and I had duty every third weekend. Sandra and I would save what little money we had so I could pay fourteen dollars for another machinist's mate to stand by, or cover, for me on a duty weekend. That gave us a little extra time together.

My TAD to the firerooms ended, and I was assigned to the Number 2 shaft alley again with Dave. The shaft alley is the last point of the ship before the shaft from the main engine leaves the ship. We had to chip, grind, and repaint areas that showed rust—and the whole damn ship was a WWII rust bucket with numerous coats of navy-gray lead paint. But it was good duty away from the engine room. Out of sight, out of mind.

I'd take the fireman's training manual down to the shaft alleys so I could study for the E-3 fireman's test. I'd question Dave about the systems and operations of the engine room and boiler room to prepare myself.

March 1968

The first week of March, Mr. Schmuck called for a seabag inspection—more harassment. In my four years aboard the *Hancock*, I had two seabag inspections, both the directives of Mr. Schmuck. Everybody was required to lay out their entire seabag on their rack so it could be inspected during the day. If you were missing a piece of clothing or a pair of shoes, you would be forced to replace it. I was always squared away, so this was not a problem for me—or so I thought.

As it turned out, my first-class petty officer notified me that I had only one pair of dress shoes and that I had until the next payday to buy a second pair. However, when I laid my seabag out on my rack that morning, I had two pairs of dress shoes, which I had received in boot camp.

Confused, I went up to the berthing compartment to check my rack. Sure enough, one pair of dress shoes were missing. The third-class petty officer in charge of the cleaning department informed me that only he and the M Division officer were allowed in the berth compartment. He generously offered to help me look for the missing shoes. We searched high and low but never found them. I was out a pair of dress shoes. Making only sixty dollars a month, Sandra and I hadn't planned on this expense.

Later, in the middle of my first deployment, the same third-class petty officer was preparing to fly off the ship at 0000 for discharge to the States, having served his four years. He was sitting at the table in the berthing area, polishing his shoes.

As I walked by, I noticed that his shoes looked brand new, considering he'd been in the navy for four years. I glanced at the initials stenciled on the inside of the shoe placed on the table: JDL. He was polishing *my* shoes! The ones he had stolen when my seabag was laid out for inspection. The ones he had "helped" me look for.

His stealing my shoes didn't surprise me. He was an untrustworthy, self-centered, disloyal adulterer and an SOB to work for. I was still a non-rate, though, so calling him out could make it hard for me. Even though he was leaving, he still had friends on the ship that could make my life beyond miserable. Being street-smart paid dividends.

So, I let it go—another day and another learning experience in the navy.

April 1968

The first week of April, I had TAD at the firefighters' school at Treasure Island Naval Base. This was a full week of intense firefighting instruction preparing the young sailors for shipboard fires. Fire on a warship is a sailor's worse nightmare.

The morning of April 5, I was riding over to Treasure Island on the military bus. The driver had the radio on, and a news flash interrupted the station with the announcement that Dr. Martin Luther King Jr. had been assassinated.

About the third week of April, the *Hancock* left the shipyards at Hunters Point for a shakedown cruise after eight months in the yard for a major overhaul. The ship was now on port and starboard duty, meaning duty every other day when in port.

This was my first time at sea. With little knowledge of the engine room or operation of equipment, my first duties were to stand messenger watch and keep the engine room clean. At nineteen years old, I had an appreciation for mechanical machinery, but again, this was overwhelming. So many different systems and individual pieces of equipment needed to come to life before the steam turbines were ready to answer commands from the bridge to get underway. However, I was looking forward to the challenge.

Note: Sandra and I wrote each other most everyday while I was at sea. As my story continues, I'll share excerpts from my letters as well as add stories of my memories at sea and during combat operation while deployed to Vietnam.

April 26, 1968

Dear Sandra,

There was black oil in the aft engine room bilges that I had to emulsify before it could be pumped over the side. I was opening and pouring five-gallon containers of chemicals into the bilges when I slipped on the oily deck plates and spilled the chemicals over the lower part of my body. I quickly made my way to the showers and washed off the chemicals.

Underway on the shakedown cruise, the USS *Hancock* passed under the Golden Gate Bridge as she headed out to sea. After a day of normal steaming, the captain ordered general quarters, which means all hands must be at battle stations. It was an organized movement of 3,200 sailors heading up starboard and down port.

I quickly made way to my general quarters station in the aft engine room. I was assigned to a headset stationed close to the top watch. Top watch was the title given to the sailor responsible for the operation of the engine room while at sea and during general quarters. In this case, the top watch was a seasoned first-class petty officer.

Once all general quarters stations were manned in the engine room, the main hatch was closed and dogged down. This meant there was no ingress or egress to the engine room. This was my first experience of watching that large, thick iron hatch close at the top of the engine room ladder and tightly dogged, or fastened.

In the picture below, the iron hatch has ten dog-ears. Once the hatch was closed, the top watch tightly secured these ten dog-ears. He'd hit each dog-ear with a ten-pound hammer, ensuring the hatch could not flail open during a disaster in the engine room.

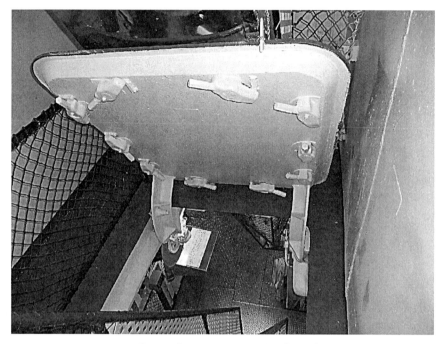

Aft engine room main hatch

We were truly locked down in the "hole" now. And I have to say, I was apprehensive. *Holy shit,* I thought. *This is real!*

The main hatch to the engine room could not be opened without permission from the bridge. We were locked in the steel walls of a compartment below the waterline with two main engines driven by 600 psi of steam at a superheated temperature of 850 degrees. I was aware that a mechanical failure and/or an operational error by the top watch would make this engineering compartment my coffin.

The ship was now operating at flank speed, maintaining thirty-two knots. The engine room was very noisy and slightly shaking with all systems operating at capacity and the two main steam turbines producing maximum horsepower. Above all, there was the noise of the 600-psi steam rushing through the steam lines to the high-pressure turbine. I can still hear it in my ears today—it's called tinnitus.

Orders were received from the bridge to reduce speed. This meant closing the throttles and reducing steam to the turbines to maintain a 115 shaft rpm. Via manual control, makeup feed water had to be immediately reduced in order to maintain proper level in the de-aerating (DA) tank. Feed water for the boilers was stored in the DA tank, which contained 4,000 gallons of water at 260 degrees at 15 psi. If the DA tank burst due to excessive pressure, the 4,000 gallons of water would instantly flash to steam, killing all those in the engine room with screams of death.

Suddenly, I realized there was an emergency. The water level in the DA tank had risen out of site in the gauge glass. Immediately, the top watch secured the makeup feed water—but it was too late.

Without warning, the safety valve on the tank lifted due to the excessive pressure in the DA tank. It produced a very deep, loud noise. It scared the living shit out of me. You'll never forget the first time you hear the sound of this safety-lifting. Especially when it's your first time in a compartment sealed off with no way out!

The top watch appeared very concerned and stressed as he and the assistant top watch managed the engine room systems and equipment to correct the emergency. This shakedown cruise was the first time the ship's engine room had been operational since July 1967. And even these seasoned petty officers were a little rusty when it came to the sequence of procedures.

For me watching it all, this was an oh-shit moment. This was a danger that could turn into a nightmare. It was scary, and I was scared.

DA tank

This incident left a mental effect on me. On that very first day at sea, I realized that operational knowledge of the engine room is the difference between life and death during casualty control and emergency situations. The deep, loud noise of the safety lift had a lasting effect on me too. Today, any un-expected noise still makes me jump out of my shoes.

Below are numerous examples of deadly engine and boiler room accidents that took place in the confined engineering compartments of naval ships deployed during the Vietnam War. Be advised I've included details that help you, the reader, understand and imagine the horror those sailors experienced before death. These details also help you understand the mental challenges still faced by those who survived such horrifying experiences. It's something they relive throughout their lives.

- April 13, 1965: The USS *Ranger* suffered a fire in the Number 1 engine room, killing one sailor. My brother Olaf worked with a sailor who escaped this fire.
- December 6, 1965: the USS *Kitty Hawk*'s Number 3 boiler room experienced a flash fire, suffocating two sailors.
- October 26, 1966: On the USS *Oriskany,* a fire started in a magnesium flare storage locker when a sailor accidentally dropped a flare. The fire spread to a nearby stock of ordinance. Below decks, spaces were soon filled with screams and shouts of trapped and dying sailors. Forty-four sailors were killed, and another thirty-eight were injured.
- June 22, 1967: the USS *Raleigh* suffered an engine room steam accident, killing two sailors.
- June 28, 1971: The main guarding valve in the USS *Trenton*'s engine room ruptured. Four sailors died on site, and six were burned, with two dying later from their burns. These sailors were most likely cooked alive like lobsters. Their skin started to fall off. They screamed in horror. As they fell to the deck plates, they took their last breath of the high-temperature steam that cooked their lungs.
- October 1, 1972: the USS *Saratoga* suffered a fire in the Number 2 engine room, killing three sailors and injuring twelve.

- February 5, 1973: A boiler room explosion in the aft engine room on the USS *Basilone* killed seven and injured four. Probably instant death—no time to react. However, the memory of removing the bodies cooked like lobsters was forever ingrained in the minds of those sailors who served with the shipmates lost.
- December 11, 1973: The USS *Kitty Hawk* experienced a blaze in the Number 1 machinery room. Seven sailors were killed and thirty-eight were injured. Their lungs filled with smoke, they choked in horror for air, and their skin roasted and charred.

Vietnam, October 26, 1966: *USS* Oriskany *engulfed in flame and smoke*

One more thought: During the war, the news media was embedded with American ground troops in Vietnam. The coverage was fed back to the homeland and broadcast over the nightly news. The naval ships were different. There was no media embedded with the ships at sea, and only limited coverage of injuries and deaths was fed back to the homeland. These deaths at sea weren't mourned by our nation.

There were over 3,200 sailors serving aboard the USS *Hancock*. Their knowledge, experience, discipline, and attention to equipment and system operation was of the utmost importance for ensuring safe operating conditions and a successful mission. Again, one sailor could jeopardize the safety and well-being of all those aboard the ship.

As I look back at the number of engine room disasters that occurred aboard other ships during the Vietnam War, I'm fortunate that I didn't experience a career-ending—or life-ending—moment. I can't stress enough that operation of the engine and boiler room was constant "controlled danger" that could become an uncontrolled life-threatening situation in an instant.

May 2, 1968
Dear Sandra,

The ship pulled into San Diego today. The Number 2 low-pressure turbine broke down. It hasn't been determined what the problem is or how serious the problem is yet. Scuttlebutt is that this could extend our time in the States.

The yardbirds pulled the inspection covers off the low-pressure turbine. They couldn't see any problems with the turbine blading or bearings. They are thinking it might be either the reduction gears or a warped shaft. My chance to view the low-pressure turbine through the inspect holes was definitely a learning experience.

I was cross-connecting the main steam, and the valve wheel was so hot I burned my fingers—big blisters. The air temperature is 120 degrees in the engine room and very humid.

May 6, 1968
Dear Sandra,

Pulled out of San Diego at 0820. General quarters was sounded from 1000 to 1415.

We were fed C rations for lunch. I traded my two small packs of cigarettes for another sailor's piece of candy.

May 8, 1968
Dear Sandra,

General quarters was sounded early this morning. I manned my GQ station and headset near the top watch. It seemed like every time you turned around, something was going wrong. They blew the safety on the DA tank twice. It scared the shit out of me again. Number 3 generator broke down, and they can't fix it until the ship pulls into port.

I don't know—if there was any way I could get out of the navy, I would. It's not worth working your ass off and not knowing what's going to happen next in the hole.

May 13, 1968
Dear Sandra,

I passed the E-3 fireman test. I had the highest score of those taking the test this month. I'm now qualified on bearing and messenger watch.

I have five dollars in my pocket to bring home from this underway training cruise.

May 22, 1968

The nuclear submarine USS *Scorpion* (SSN-589) sank, and all ninety-nine sailors aboard were killed. My research indicates that the navy describes the loss of the *Scorpion* as an "unexplained catastrophic event."

The USS Scorpion

June 5, 1968

Sandra and I were over at Marie and Floyd's for dinner when breaking news came on TV that Robert Kennedy had been shot and killed. Kennedy had been campaigning in California for president when he was assassinated. Hubert Humphrey became the Democratic Party nominee for president later that summer.

June 13, 1968

Dear Sandra,

I've been training to stand throttle watch, and I just passed the written and skills test. I'm now qualified and standing throttle watch alone.

June 15, 1968

Dear Sandra,

The ship is underway conducting sea exercises. A lieutenant junior grade (LTJG) catapulted off the ship, and his F8 jet experienced an explosion and flameout. He ejected and was recovered.

The Hancock *was the first United States aircraft carrier equipped with steam catapults and an angled deck, allowing the launch and recovery of jet aircraft. I believe pilots launched and recovered from this old WWII Essex-class aircraft carrier had ice water pumping through their veins— nerves of steel!*

F8 catapult launch

June to Early July 1968

My first deployment date of July 18 was fast approaching. During the months of May and June, the ship had been in and out of port conducting sea trials, operational-readiness drills, and general quarters.

The beginning of July, the captain ordered port and starboard duty, meaning there was duty every other day. I was now home only every other night and had duty every other weekend. Our time together had diminished. Sandra and I were feeling the stress as the date for deployment neared.

Chapter 6

Operation Rolling Thunder

USS Hancock *deploying from Hawaii to Vietnam on July 31, 1968.*

The USS *Hancock* was set to deploy in July 1968 to join Task Force Seventy-Seven in Operation Rolling Thunder. Authorized by President Johnson, Operation Rolling Thunder started in March 1965, after the Gulf of Tonkin incident in 1964. It was a massive bombing campaign of North Vietnam intended to put military pressure on the North Vietnamese Communist leaders and reduce their capacity to wage war against South Vietnam and the United States. Research shows that millions of tons of bombs were dropped on North Vietnam from March 1965 to October 1968.

However, the campaign had little effect. As discussed in

chapter 1, this was because the White House, not the generals and admirals, controlled the prosecution of the war. Specific and major targets of importance often came directly from the White House or the secretary of defense's office. Targets such as trucks and oil barges were left to the admirals overseeing Task Force Seventy-Seven. Normally, naval combat operations are the duty of the Pacific fleet commander, a four-star admiral schooled in naval warfare.

A major reason why the Johnson administration could not win the war was due to their so-called rules of engagement. Case in point:

1. Pilots were not allowed to fly within thirty nautical miles of the border with Communist China. Well, guess where the VC staged the equipment and attacks from? You're right—where US pilots were not allowed to fly.

2. Our pilots were ordered not to attack the North Vietnamese foreign embassies or kill government leaders. Why? Because the administration hoped to negotiate a solution to the war and did not want the North Vietnamese leaders dead.

3. Our pilots were prohibited from attacking Hanoi, nor could they strike within a thirty-mile radius of the city.

4. Our pilots were ordered not to attack a four-nautical-mile zone around the heart of Haiphong, the chief seaport, in order to avoid Soviet, Chinese, and other merchant ships. (Which all supplied food and arms to the North Vietnamese.) They also could not strike within a ten-mile radius of

Haiphong.

5. Our pilots could not strike communist anti-aircraft artillery or surface-to-air missile sites unless the enemy fired first.

Thanks to these rules of engagement restricting our own bombing campaign, North Vietnam used the off-limits areas as sanctuaries to stockpile mass amounts of weapons, ammunition, military supplies, and raw material. Johnson handicapped our "flowering youth" (his words, not mine), spilled blood, and wasted treasure.

As I approached my first deployment to join Operation Rolling Thunder, little did I realize I was one of the young men used as a pawn in this political war.

Early July 1968

Your first deployment isn't something you can prepare for. There isn't a book you can read. Nor have you experienced, at such a young age, anything close to what you're about to embark on.

Adding to it all, my best friend and mentor, Dave, had been discharged from the navy. It was a heartfelt loss of a shipmate and a friend as I prepared to deploy. This was a person who took me under his arm, shielded me from harassment, guided me morally, and gave me a sound professional foundation upon which to build in the aft engine room.

As deployment approached, we lived day by day. Sandra was pregnant with Heide. I was now nineteen years old and an E-3 fireman who had much on his plate to manage. I was in the process of qualifying for various watches in the engine room; learning the operation, systems, and equipment of the engine room; studying for the E-4 noncommissioned officer's military requirement exam; and working long hours in miserable conditions preparing for deployment. The engine and boiler rooms were now in operational condition, and these engineering compartments were extremely warm.

July 18, 1968

My cousin Marie gave us a ride, first dropping Sandra off at the airport. She was heading back to Minnesota to live with her parents during my deployment. Marie then dropped me off at the Alameda naval station main gate.

My only memory of that morning was the walk from the main gate to where the ship was moored—long and lonely with a feeling of emptiness and loss. The ship was scheduled for an eight-month deployment. At the time, it seemed like eternity.

July 19, 1968

Dear Sandra,

Saying goodbye to you was heartbreaking. I quietly cried myself to sleep. Knowing this is my first deployment to Vietnam is gut-wrenching. And knowing we have two more deployments before my discharge from the navy—I don't have the words to express my feelings.

Today, Americans watch on television as military personnel are separated from their families. Most viewers have no idea the pain and stress the military families experience. Unless you have experienced it, I don't believe you can fully grasp the emotions involved. Military families give the fullest for their country.

July 20, 1968

Dear Sandra,

The ship sailed out of Alameda naval air station this morning and is underway for Vietnam. We'll join Task Force

Seventy-Seven to provide combat operation from the South China Sea, a location known as Yankee Station. The ship's crew received numerous shots today to prepare for overseas travel.

Just like in boot camp, these shots were with air guns and needles. As I lined up and walked through sick bay, there was a corpsman on each side of me. One held the air gun tight against your arm and pulled the trigger, and the other corpsmen stuck you with a needle. Then you'd walk away. The pain would hit about the time you exited into the passageway outside of sick bay. It was another oh-shit moment. The air guns really stung.

July 21, 1968
Dear Sandra,

The engine rooms are now 120 degrees, making working conditions and standing watch miserable in the extreme heat. My clothes are soaked with sweat when leaving the engine room. I'm standing throttle watch on Number 3 throttle.

I went up to take a shower after standing the 0000–0400 watch and found that some son of a bitch laid a big pile of shit in one of the shower stalls.

We called this guy the phantom shitter. Throughout the remainder of my first cruise, the phantom shitter would shit in the shower stalls. Sometimes he'd set his shit in various places, such as in a soap tray, in overhead air ducts, pipes, ledges, and so on. I can picture this guy as one of the military's finest. The master-at-arms (cops on the ship) tried catching this sicko but never did. It only happened on my first cruise, though, so it must have been his last deployment.

July 22, 1968

Dear Sandra,

The ship is approaching Hawaii. The outside air temperature is warmer, as is the seawater temperature. This makes the engine room even more miserable. The captain ordered tropical hours, meaning the ship's crew does not have to turn to (work) when not on watch.

M Division is short on personnel, so I'm standing watch four hours on and four hours off at sea. As a non-rate, I'm also required to man the working parties, bringing aboard food and bombs when assigned. I end a four-hour watch, and then I'm assigned to a working party an hour later. All I'm doing is eating, sleeping, reporting to working parties, and standing watch. Unloading bombs in the hanger bay in 90-degree heat felt comfortable after coming out of the 120-degree heat in the engine room! But I'm so tired.

I have a military pay stub that shows a net of $60.88 per month, and I was working an average of 540 to 600 hours per month when at sea. This equals about 0.11 cents per hour. Oh, and I got free room and board!

July 23, 1968

Dear Sandra,

It's sinking in that this is my life for the next eight months. I long to hold you.

July 27, 1968

Dear Sandra,

I have three years left in the navy. It was a year ago that I left for boot camp—so much has happened. The ship pulled out of Hawaii to conduct operational readiness inspection drills. But during the drills, we lost a plane, and the pilot was

lost at sea. Also, a sailor fell overboard. A "man overboard"
alert was sounded, requiring everyone to muster at their
duty stations. My duty station is the aft engine room. The
ship never slowed down. Our destroyer escort, along with a
helicopter, conducted the search. I don't know if a recovery
was made.

I was called up to sick bay today to receive three more
shots. After receiving the shots, I walked fifty feet, and
suddenly it felt like I had been shot in the arm with a .22
revolver!

July 31, 1968

At a ceremony aboard the USS *Hancock*, Admiral John McCain II—father of the now-deceased Senator John McCain III—became commander in chief of the Pacific fleet. This was a big event for the USS *Hancock*. As I look back, I take pride in having served on the *Hancock* during this important military change of command and in having served in the Seventh Fleet under Admiral McCain's leadership.

As Admiral McCain took over as commander, his son was experiencing brutal conditions as a prisoner of war (POW) in North Vietnam. John McCain had been shot down and captured during a bombing mission over Vietnam in October 1967. He remained a POW until 1973, when all the POWs were released.

I suggest everyone read *Faith of My Fathers: A Family Memoir* by Senator McCain. War is hell, and this book describes the experiences of a father in charge of the Pacific fleet and a son being held captive as a POW. I still have strong feelings for Admiral McCain, and I voted for Senator McCain for president of the United States in 2008—two strong men of my era who gave all to their country.

August 2, 1968

Dear Sandra,

I was standing throttle watch on Number 3 throttle today, and I had to complete several qualification drills to demonstrate my knowledge and ability to operate a ship's main engine. One of the drills required you to take the main engine shaft from 100 rpm to zero as quickly as possible. First you had to stop the shaft from turning, then you had to hold it and keep it from free-wheeling, due to the external force of the water pushing against the screw. My time was fifteen seconds, which is considered very good.

The ship's largest evaporator broke down and is out of commission. The ship is on mild water hours, meaning showers can only be taken during specified times of the day. Also, we have to take a seamen's shower—wet down, soap down, and rinse down. Anyone caught running the water continuously would be written up and sent to captain's mast. Working in the hot engine room, not being able to shower after standing watch, and sleeping in close quarters makes for an unpleasant environment. Having received fresh commissary in Hawaii, the chow is about the only thing to look forward to.

The chow hall situation only added to that unpleasant environment. When the ship was in port, the food had been good—sometimes very good. But after a week or so at sea, the food turned to shit. If a food could be condensed to powder, they did it: powdered milk, powdered eggs, powdered cottage cheese, powered potatoes, and so on.

Even when good food was being served, there were times you'd pass because of how it was prepared and/or served. I remember going through the chow line for breakfast, and there was a third-class cook frying eggs to order. He was short and fat, hunched over the grill half-asleep, and dripping sweat onto the grill. It wasn't an appetizing or mouthwatering moment.

As I approached him with my metal tray in hand, he looked up with his eyes half-closed and in a gruff voice asked, "How you want your eggs?"

"Forget it," I said. As I walked away, I found that his demeanor matched his appearance.

I often thought about that guy. If there had been an emergency and he had to escape through a scuttle opening, he would have died, as would have those waiting behind him. He was so overweight that he never would have fit through an escape scuttle opening.

August 6, 1968
Dear Sandra,

I have an infection in my foot. Sick bay gave me a no-duty chit and orders to stay off my foot, keep a warm towel on it, and report back at 1830. I don't know where they think I'm going to get a warm towel. There's hardly any water to take a shower. Sick bay said if the infection doesn't improve, they'll have to cut the infection out.

The ship crossed the International Date Line. I'm now considered a dragonback. Whoopee! They reset the ship's time, turning the clocks ahead twenty-four hours. Skipped a complete day in my life. One less day I have to suffer.

The captain came over the closed-circuit TV and said we'll arrive back in the States the first week of March 1969.

August 8, 1968
Dear Sandra,

Now my right ankle and leg are swollen. It's red, it hurts, and I can hardly walk on it.

Mr. Schmuck was in one of his asshole moods and had everyone turning to, even though the captain has ordered tropical working hours. I had to wire-brush the hot deck plates on my hands and knees. I didn't say anything about my ankle because I knew he wouldn't provide a light-duty chit. Wire-brushing the hot deck plates is a bunch of bullshit. Non-rates are standing watch four hours on and four hours off, twenty-four hours a day, seven days a week—plus mustering for working parties. I worked all day on my hands and knees on hot deck plates in 120-degree heat. It was miserable, and I was soaked with sweat.

On the tenth, the ship is pulling into Yokosuka, Japan, for three days. The ship is on port and starboard duty, so I'll have only one day off. I'm looking forward to catching up on sleep and studying for my third-class military requirements test.

Counting the days left in the Navy: 1088.

August 9, 1968

Dear Sandra,

The ship is heading toward Japan, and I'm standing watch on Number 3 throttle. The ship was in the process of pulling alongside an oiler to replenish the Number 6 black oil [note: Number 6 black oil is used to fire the boilers and generate steam for the main engines] *when an unidentified plane was spotted on radar. The captain ordered an emergency breakaway. I went from an uneventful shaft speed of 33 rpm to an all-ahead full and then to an all-ahead flank and an rpm of over 200. I've only been qualified on throttles for two months, and I knew this wasn't normal procedure. The top watch informed me the flight deck was preparing for launch and to stay alert. My heart was pounding as I responded to the telegraph orders from the* bridge. I opened the ahead throttle valve dragging main steam from the boilers down to 585 psi. However, I was unable to reach flank rpm until the Number 3 boiler room added maximum burners to the Number 5 and Number 6 boilers.

The captain required flank speed to increase the airspeed across the flight deck to ensure a successful launch of two F-8 fighter jets that were in ready status on the ship's catapults. The F-8 jets were launched to intercept the unidentified plane approaching. The aircraft was then identified as a Russian bomber called "the Big Bear." It's not uncommon for the Russians to harass United States military ships.

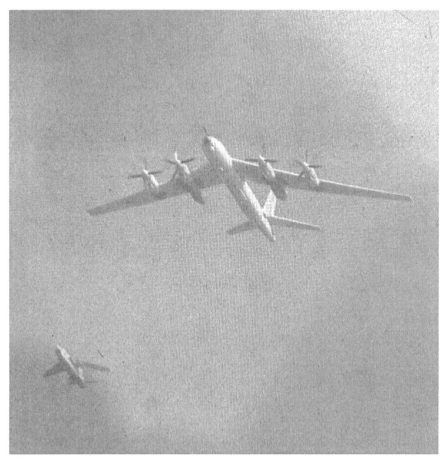

F-8 jet (left) from the USS Hancock *escorting a Russian bomber*

If you have seen the movie *Top Gun*, you might remember the scene at the end when Tom Cruise is catapulted off the USS *Enterprise* to intercept several Russian jets moving toward the carrier. The movie showed the intense moments aboard the ship and in the air.

Not only did I actually live this same type of event in "real time" aboard the ship, but I was *part* of it, standing throttle watch on the Number 3 main engine. And understand, I had been in the navy for only one year when this happened. I was nineteen years old and in control of one of the ship's four screws and a 37,500-horsepower main engine. I received commands from the bridge and was responsible for performing as trained with no errors. I remember this successful event as intense and exhilarating—another huge adrenaline rush!

Our pilots intercepted and escorted the aircraft to ensure there was no threat to the carrier or the task force.

August 10, 1968
Dear Sandra,

The ship pulled into Yokosuka today. I don't plan to leave the ship, except to buy a sandwich on the pier. Most people from M Division who have liberty are going into Yokosuka to hit the bars and get drunk.

August 12, 1968
Dear Sandra,

The ship is back to sea and heading for Vietnam. The ship will join Task Force Seventy-Seven in the Gulf of Tonkin, called Yankee Station, and participate in a bombing campaign called Operation Rolling Thunder.

One hundred thousand gallons of black oil was determined to be no good, and the boiler technicians were ordered to pump it over the side.

The landing gear on an A-4 would not drop, and the jet landed on its underside as it slid into a barrier net. The pilot walked away without any injuries.

August 19, 1968
Dear Sandra,

The Hancock *lost her first plane in theater today to the*

South China Sea. The plane's hydraulic system failed and led to an out-of-control F-8 fighter jet. The pilot ejected and broke his leg but was rescued.

August 22, 1968
Dear Sandra,
I was assigned to a working party bringing aboard 250- and 500-pound bombs. Alongside a supply ammunitions ship, my job was to remove the bombs from their tin pallets, load them on carts, and deliver them to the bomb bay's elevators.
Also, I found out an E-3 with a child receives another $30/month. So, when the baby is born, send me a copy of the birth certificate.

August 24, 1968
Dear Sandra,
The Hancock *continues flying bombing mission over Vietnam. Our pilots blew up a couple trucks and a bridge today, and they're going after a couple barges filled with oil tomorrow. I'm now part of the Vietnam War.*

August 27, 1968
Dear Sandra,
The ship was ordered on water hours again. The 100,000-gallon-per-day evaporator is out of commission. We haven't been given a timeline for repairs to be completed. Life aboard the ship had already become very demanding—now this!

August 29, 1968
Dear Sandra,
The ship is still on water hours. I'm looking forward 181

days, when the ship will return to the States. I'm counting down!

August 30, 1968
Dear Sandra,
I was watching flight operations on the 07 level and getting some fresh air. A two-engine prop job (an airplane with propellers) landed, hitting the deck hard, and blew out a tire—interesting moment. Also, an A-4 jet was shot down by the VC today. Our pilot bailed out and landed in a heavily wooded area. A helicopter recovered the pilot before the North Vietnamese captured him. Rescue helicopters are first out and last to land during flight operations.

August 31, 1968
Dear Sandra,
We were steaming in the Gulf of Tonkin, and an F-8 returning from combat operations crashed while trying to land on the carrier. The pilot was killed.

The pilot, a lieutenant commander (LCDR), had dropped below his sink point and crashed into the back of ship, what is known as the fantail. The plane split in two and exploded. The LCDR's body was never recovered.

The LCDR had graduated from the US Naval Academy in 1958. He had gotten married the same year and began a family. His wife, Barbara, said their marriage was right out of a storybook. She later said it was a "happily-ever-after dream."

September 4, 1968
Dear Sandra,
I was just relieved from watch. I didn't write yesterday because I worked twenty-two hours straight before I hit my

rack for four hours of sleep. The harsh working conditions and operational demands push a sailor's mental and physical stamina close to a breaking point.

To top off yesterday, I received the package you sent. I know it was sent with love—thank you. However, it took fourteen days to get here. The brownies were reduced to crumbs that were like small rocks.

A squadron of jets with bombs flies strikes off the ship and returns in about an hour with no bombs. This goes on for twelve hours every day the ship is online. The next twelve hours of the twenty-four-hour period, the ship pulls alongside a supply ship to receive food, fuel, and bombs.

The good news: because of my qualification on throttle watch, I'm dodging a lot of working parties. The bad news: standing four hours on, four hours off makes for a long twenty-four hours, especially if you catch a working party or if repairs are needed in aft engine room. War at sea is a dog's life! In fact, a damn dog has a better life than an E-3 fireman in the engine room.

While I'm complaining, the food has turned to shit at sea. I'm losing weight not only due to sweating but also because the food is garbage.

Our first class is having nightmares again. The engine room is really getting to him. Remember back in the States when he took the liberty launch from Hunters Point to the Alameda naval station, and he forgot he drove that day? So, when the liberty launch got to the Alameda naval station, he and those planning to ride with him (including me) had to walk home because his car was at Hunters Point. Anyway, his responsibilities weigh heavy on his shoulders. He's responsible for the operation, repair, and maintenance of the aft engine room and the safety of those sailors in the engine room. The pressure from the asshole Mr. Schmuck has put him over the edge.

The ship is scheduled to pull into the Philippine Islands (PIs) on September 6, another first for me. It took me eighteen years to leave Minnesota. But now I'm nineteen years old, and the PIs will be the second foreign port I've visited in the last two months. "Join the navy and see the world!" But what they didn't tell you is that your life would be worse than a dog's!

As I look back, I remember how Mr. Schmuck ordered the first class to direct and supervise tasks of his crew in the engine room. It was just short of abuse, causing heartache for the first class, who was obligated to follow orders given by an officer.

Please keep in mind the military is not a democratic organization. It's dictatorial. It's managed with the understanding that the person with superior rank is in charge and that those reporting to that person will carry out all orders given. There's no debate. When a superior was in a bad mood, his reports suffered.

September 6, 1968
Dear Sandra,

The ship is in port, and I have the 1600 to 2000 messenger watch in port. One of the duties as messenger in the aft engine room is to check the port and starboard shaft alley every hour to ensure the water level is kept at a minimum. The shaft of the Number 2 and 3 main engines exits the back of the ship through stern tubes. The stern tubes are filled with packing, called a packing gland. The packing gland requires a small amount of "leak-off" (seawater) to lubricate the shaft when turning. The seawater coming into the shaft alley needs to be pumped out to ensure the shaft alley doesn't flood.

So I climbed down four decks and through the hatch of the Number 2 shaft alley—it was flooded. The spring bearings supporting the shaft were under water, as was the electric JP-5 pump used for transferring jet fuel. This wasn't good. It was another oh-shit moment.

I reported back to my second-class section leader and informed him of the situation. The messenger watch standing the 1200 to 1600 duty—a friend of mine—hadn't checked the shaft alley during his four-hour watch. It caused a big problem.

My second-class section leader instructed me to say nothing. He didn't want anybody to get in trouble. If Mr. Schmuck found out, he'd have those involved punished with miserable work detail.

I was instructed to pump the shaft alley ASAP. I lined up the necessary valving to take a suction on the flooded shaft alley. After I pumped the seawater out, the second class and I spent the next several hours, beyond our watch, draining all the oil out of both spring bearings and refilling with new oil.

As for the JP-5 pump, we didn't inform the aviation crew of the situation. However, I'm sure the next time they started the pump to transfer fuel, it blew up in smoke.

My friend was lucky—he could have been written up for dereliction of duty, and he could have ended up at captain's mast.

September 7, 1968

Dear Sandra,

It's the ship's second day in the PIs. We're standing two-section duty, and tomorrow is my day off in port. I was planning on sleeping in, studying, and purchasing some *edible food on the pier. However, our first class called for a muster in the engine room at 0800 and turn-to. Mr. Schmuck is coming down to inspect the engine room to make sure everybody is working. This type of bullshit is the reason our first class is having nightmares, and it hurts morale. Anyway, liberty call is now at 1600. So, I'll have fourteen hours to study and catch up on sleep instead of twenty-four hours.*

Liberty in the PIs means bars, drinking, prostitutes, and fights for the sailors who have been confined to the ship for the last thirty days, living in substandard conditions and working sixteen to twenty hours a day under extreme conditions. The sailors go over on liberty and come back financially broke, drunk, vomiting, black-and-blue from fights, and there's a good possibility that they caught a case of the clap (VD) too. The berthing compartment, where I'm trying to sleep, stinks of puke. It's noisy, and the drunken sailors turned the lights on. And being a non-rate on the bottom rack is the worst place to be. What a fucking mess, son of a bitch! And to top it off, in a week or so, the same sailors will be in a long line leading to sick bay because their lower units have started to drip from VD. All I wanted was a good night's sleep!

September 8, 1968

Dear Sandra,

The heel came off my work boot, and new pair of boots are $30. So the money I send you this month will be less. Sorry.

The ship is pulling out of the PIs on the morning of the ninth—that is, if the yardbirds can finish making repairs to the radar system that was damaged when an F-8 crash-landed at the end of our last line period.

September 9, 1968

Dear Sandra,

The ship is pulling out of the PIs and heading for Yankee Station to rejoin Task Force Seventy-Seven and Operation Rolling Thunder.

September 12, 1968

Dear Sandra,

We're on Yankee Station, and the Captain informed the crew that this line period will be thirty days. I'm standing four hours on and four hours off in the extreme heat. That plus assigned working parties will make for a long line period.

A frightening moment occurred today when the Number 2 electrical switchboard blew up in the aft engine room. Luckily, no one was hurt. We lost all lights, electric pumps, and the ventilation system serving the engine room. The top watch was scrambling to ensure that all necessary systems were operational, that main engines were maintaining vacuum, and that the main engines didn't have to be shut down. The only lights were emergency battery-operated light packs, leaving the poorly lit engine room difficult to operate and even more dangerous. Though, I wasn't as scared this time—I'm getting a little more confrontable during emergencies.

Several hours later, the electricians were able to restore electrical power to the engine room. But until then, working conditions were dangerous, intense, and extreme as the ship continued combat operation.

With no ventilation, the engine room reached 160 degrees. We rotated watches every three to five minutes due to the extreme heat. I was called to relieve Number 3 throttle every five minutes.

The first class in charge stayed in the engine room during the entire emergency to ensure further operational readiness and the safety of his crew. There wasn't a dry piece of clothing on his body.

Due to the extreme heat, we were required to ingest salt tablets from a dispenser located in the engine rooms. I don't know if that was good or bad, but I swallowed many. They were forced on you by order of Mr. Schmuck.

I remember the air was so hot that it burned to breathe, and you could only touch metal for a second or two. You couldn't touch the hand rails on the ladder leading to and from the engine room. The ahead and astern throttle wheels were wrapped with thin rope to insulate your hands from burns. Rags were used to open and close valves.

September 14, 1968

Dear Sandra,

The captain sounded general quarters (GQ) today. My GQ station is Number 3 throttle. The main hatch to the engine room was closed and dogged down as the ship was to participate in antisubmarine warfare drills.

These drills were to test the skill and knowledge of all watches in both the forward and aft engine rooms as well as all four throttle watches controlling the main engines. We were told the purpose of this exercise was to make the aircraft carrier sound like a destroyer in the hopes of keeping an enemy submarine from pursuing us. As I think back, though, this old WWII trick was obsolete in the late 1960s. The Russian submarines were much more sophisticated at that time. Also, my research indicates that during that year, the Russians subs were starting to carry tactical nuclear torpedoes!

The captain's orders from the bridge were to stop main engines Number 2 and 3 and drag their screws, and also bring main engines Number 1 and 4 to 115 rpm. Main control (engineering officers stationed in the forward engine room and in command of all engineering operations) next ordered the aft engine room to engage the jacking gear on the Number 2 and 3 reduction gears.

The purpose of the jacking gear is to rotate the main engines, keeping the engines from warping during cooldown. The ratio of the jacking gear is 36,000 rpm to 1 rpm. Meaning, it takes the jacking gear motor 36,000 revolutions to turn the main shaft one turn. With the jacking gears engaged on the Number 2 and 3 shafts, they made one full revolution every ten minutes.

As the ship moved forward, dragging two screws, suddenly there was a very loud explosion. Chunks of metal went flying at high speed through the engine room. Most everybody about shit their pants. Another oh-shit moment! As it turned out, the Number 2 main engine shaft had rotated several full turns in a matter of seconds, causing the jacking gear motor to far exceed its designed rpm and explode.

Mr. Schmuck was the officer in charge of the aft engine room during this exercise. Not knowing exactly what had happened—other than a loud explosion—Mr. Schmuck was concerned about further damage to the Number 2 main engine. He approached me quickly and gave me an order via my headset to direct throttles Number 1 and 4 to secure forward throttles and open astern throttles to back down the ship. He also ordered the top watch to disengage the Number 3 jacking gear—my throttle.

The aft engine room crew was now in an extreme casualty-control situation. I still have a mental picture of the stressful concern on the face of the top watch as he instructed me to hold the shaft dead still as he then proceeded to move alongside the main engine to disengage the jacking gear. I now realize he was entrusting me, a green throttle watch with only a few months of experience, to be mistake-free. If I didn't do my part perfectly, another jacking gear would have been compromised with the top watch working right next to it. It could have led to severe injury or loss of life.

Once the jacking gear was disengaged, Mr. Schmuck ordered me to open astern throttle and drag the main steam to 550 psi. Again, these were extreme casualty-control measures.

Mr. Schmuck smoked a shitty old pipe. He was always sucking on it, even when it wasn't lit. I still remember him standing behind me, puffing on that shitty old pipe, as I dragged steam to 550 psi on the Number 3 throttle. It was a very tense moment. He was making more smoke than the Number 5 and 6 boilers, as the boiler operators added burners to produce maximum steam to the main engine via my throttle.

Dragging 550 psi on the boiler is a rare occurrence for a throttle watch. Unless there was an order from an officer in the engine room, the main stream pressure from the boilers was not to be dragged below 585 psi.

My adrenaline was pumping! I concentrated on the Number 3 throttle gauge panel and listened for further instructions from main control via my headset. At this point, though, I *wasn't* responding to the orders from the bridge, which added additional danger to the ship.

Mr. Schmuck's reason for this extreme and dangerous casualty-control measure was to prevent further damage to the Number 2 main engine's reduction gears. He wanted to stop forward movement of the ship, ensuring that the Number

2 shaft did not turn and do additional damage to the reduction gears, as the shaft and screw now turned freely.

Within several minutes—which seemed like hours—main control directed all throttle watches to once again follow telegraph orders from the bridge. Orders came in for ahead throttle, 115 rpm.

Looking back, I realize how close we were to disaster with the jacking gear motor explosion. Fortunately, the flying shrapnel didn't strike anyone or damage equipment. Understand, a deadly situation could have erupted if a chunk of metal had pierced a main steam line, a lube oil line, or the lube oil storage tank directly across from the jacking gear motor. Lube oil spraying or leaking onto a hot steam line can flash into a fire, creating heavy smoke and sucking up the oxygen in the compartment.

But that wasn't the only disaster nearly avoided. Mr. Schmuck didn't realize a destroyer was following directly behind the USS *Hancock* during this exercise. The scuttlebutt was that the destroyer almost rear-ended the *Hancock* when we quickly slowed forward movement and didn't relay the information to the bridge via main control. When Mr. Schmuck ordered all throttles astern with a destroyer bearing down on our stern, he put the entire *Hancock,* as well as the destroyer, in danger. I wish I could have been a mouse in the corner of the next engineering meeting, so I could have heard Mr. Schmuck explain his actions.

What caused this near casualty? The Number 2 throttle watch—without orders—opened his astern throttle with the jacking gear engaged. A big no-no! When in port and the main engine jacking gear is engaged, the throttles are chained closed and locked to ensure this type of accident doesn't happen.

This information remained a secret within the enlisted ranks in the aft engine room. The M Division officers never found out that Number 2 throttle watch had opened the astern throttle without an order from an officer, causing the explosion and damage. Had they known, he most likely would have ended up in the brig for that action.

An interesting side comment: that same sailor was later standing watch on the Number 3 generator when he saved the life of an electrician who was being electrocuted. The sailor was awarded a Naval Service Metal for saving the life of a shipmate.

September 17, 1968

Dear Sandra,
   Lost another F-8 fighter jet today.

The pilot, a lieutenant junior grade (LTJG), was in a lengthy dogfight with a MiG-21 near Vinh. His F-8 jet was running low on fuel, so the LTJG broke away and headed out to sea for aerial refueling. But as the pilot approached the tanker, his engine flamed out from fuel starvation. The pilot had to eject. A search-and-rescue (SAR) helicopter rescued him.

During my second deployment to Vietnam, this LTJG pilot would be killed as he crashed on the deck of the *Hancock*.

September 18, 1968

Dear Sandra,
   I'm having a hard time finding time to study and work on my E-4 military requirements. I need to finish the course material to be able to take the test at the end of the month.
   Word is, one of our F-8 jets was shot down by a Russian MiG flown by a North Vietnamese pilot.

I went up to the 07 level today for a little sunshine and watched A-4 jets launch from the ship fully loaded with bombs under their wings. Thirty minutes later, the planes returned with no bombs. It was a constant launch and retrieval of aircraft. This choreographed assault against the enemy occurs twelve hours a day, every day, during a thirty-day line period. With three aircraft carriers on the line launching bombing assaults against the enemy, you'd think the war would be short lived. The ship is steaming about one hundred miles off the coast of Vietnam.

September 20, 1968
Dear Sandra,

The captain sounded GQ for one hour today for the purpose of keeping the crew trained in GQ and casualty-control procedures. Luckily, I was already on watch, so it didn't interrupt my sleep.

There's a machinist's mate stationed in the forward engine room who wasn't showering, who wore his dirty socks to bed, who hadn't changed his underwear, and so on. So a couple of disgruntled shipmates pulled him out of his rack, manhandled him up to the showers, stripped him of his underwear and socks, and verbally and physically persuaded him to clean up and stay clean.

September 22, 1968
Dear Sandra,

Word is, the nuclear cruiser USS Long Beach *shot down a Russian MiG with a guided surface-to-air Talos missile. The North Vietnamese pilot was probably trying to sneak out to sea toward the carrier task force for a surprise attack on a ship.*

Think about it: this North Vietnamese pilot wasn't out on a Sunday joyride in his Russian MiG, and he wasn't lost. No, he had received orders from his North Vietnamese superiors to make a sneak attack. He was probably thinking, *Oh, shit. Why me?*

Think about it too: as part of Johnson's rules of engagement, US forces could not engage North Vietnamese MiGs unless they crossed a longitude and latitude predetermined by the White House. Such rules limited our military options to fight and win the war.

Research shows that the USS *Long Beach* shot down two MiGs with surface-to-air missiles while deployed to Vietnam. The first MiG was at the range of sixty-five miles, and the second was at a range of sixty-one miles. The Yankee Station operating area was about one hundred miles off the coast, in the Gulf of Tonkin at 16 degrees north latitude, 110 degrees east longitude.

I'm convinced these North Vietnamese pilots were trying to penetrate the carrier task force defenses to strike a US warship in the Gulf of Tonkin. There were two to three aircraft carriers in the gulf at all times. At sixty-five miles, these North Vietnamese pilots were closing in on the strike range window.

USS Long Beach *launching a surface-to-air missile*

In 1968, this young sailor in the engine room never considered that such external dangers abounded. I look back now and realize that the risk of a MiG airstrike was very low. But I also realize that a successful strike would have caused severe damage to a ship and casualties to its crew. It would have been a momentum builder for the enemy.

Thankfully, carrier sailors such as myself never saw a MiG during the Vietnam War. We were provided excellent air cover. At all times, fighter jets were in the air to defend the carrier task force against MiGs and torpedo boats.

Also, the Seventh Fleet set up a positive identification radar advisory zone. The US ships were equipped with the most-advanced communications and radar that could track all aircraft over North Vietnam. The system could track a North Vietnamese MiG from takeoff to landing. This radar system was a vital link for the Task Force Seventy-Seven command and control system.

September 23, 1968

Dear Sandra,

Word is, a second carrier on the line with the Hancock *had an F-8 jet crash while landing. The pilot was killed along with three enlisted sailors and an officer who were on the flight deck.*

Watching flight operation from the 07 level the other day, I saw firsthand the potential dangers in this area.

September 24, 1968

Dear Sandra,

The captain came over the main communications (1MC) and said that one of our A-4 jets had been shot down over Vietnam, and that the pilot had been captured.

Also, the ship lost a second A-4 jet today. It was hit by anti-aircraft artillery (AAA) fire while bombing a bridge eleven miles north of Vinh.

The pilot who was captured was a lieutenant commander. He was on a mission to attack river barges with Zuni rockets. A round of 37mm flak hit his A-4 Skyhawk, badly injuring his leg and knocking him temporarily unconscious. When he came to, he could not control the A-4 and had to punch out. He was held as a POW until he was released in 1973, after four and a half years of pure hell.

The second A-4 was hit north of Vinh, and the aircraft began streaming fuel. The engine flamed out just as it crossed the coast. The pilot, an LTJG, ejected a few miles offshore. A navy SH-3 helicopter picked him up.

Remember "GI Jane" Fonda? She traveled to North

Vietnam in 1972 and was welcomed by the government. She was pictured sitting on an anti-aircraft gun, looking through a sighting glass. It was the same type of anti-aircraft gun that shot down these two A-4s.

I don't hold ill will for those who protested against the war. But I do hold ill will for traitors.

September 25, 1968
Dear Sandra,

I woke up for watch and found two letters under my pillow—so happy! There's not much to be happy about at sea. In fact, nothing.

Understand, letters from Sandra were a huge mental uplift. I read them several times as I waited for the next mail call. She would also dribble a little perfume on the letters or kiss them with red lipstick, reminding me of her love. It was as close to her as I could get.

September 26, 1968
Dear Sandra,

I'm standing break-in on the 0400 to 0800 watch, qualifying on the ship service turbo generator. When the messenger came to wake me up, I was totally blank mentally. It was dark in the berthing compartment, and I didn't have any idea of what time it was, where I was, or what I was being told. My brain wouldn't engage. It was a very odd feeling.

Sleep is so hard to come by. I was up twenty-four hours with only three hours of sleep and only four hours of sleep before that. It's round-the-clock operation, and there's very little rest.

I remember that after standing watch, I would lie in my rack and wish I could just stay awake for a few minutes to think about Sandra and home. But I'd be so tired I'd fall asleep, only to be woken three and a half hours later for the next watch. I promised myself I'd never complain about not being able to sleep at night when I got out of the navy—and I don't.

September 27, 1968

Dear Sandra,

I'm rotating four hours on, four hours off, plus I'm working during the day to repair equipment, and I'm assigned to working parties bringing aboard bombs and food. Just can't get enough sleep. The engineering division has a shortage of machinist's mates.

I'm almost broken in on generator watch. The boiler rooms are hotter than the engine rooms—140 degrees on the upper level next to the air ejector. The third-class petty officer breaking me in on generator watch is from West Virginia. It's my understanding he didn't wear shoes until joining the navy. So, his feet are really nasty. He cleans and brushes them with a wire brush on generator watch—another first for me.

September 29, 1968

Dear Sandra,

I qualified for generator watch. I signed a document stating I was qualified, as did my first class. I'm now standing watch on Number 3 generator, which is located in the Number 3 boiler room. It's hot. The boiler room is 140 degrees near the generator's air ejector, where there isn't a fresh-air blower. The outside air temperature is in the midnineties anyway, so fresh air doesn't mean air conditioning.

The Number 2 switchboard blew up again in the aft engine room. They lost all lights, ventilation, and electric pumps.

The sea is really rough, and the ship is rolling a lot more than usual.

When I make E-4, my pay will increase to $238 per month. My current monthly pay as an E-3 is $137 per month.

I was only a few months into my eight-month deployment. It was miserable! Sixteen-to-twenty-hour workdays. Shit for food. Sleeping in a small berthing compartment with seventy racks stacked three or four high with a bunch of stinking sailors. The inmates in the state and federal jail system are treated better. I don't know what it's like today aboard the newer carriers, but on an old WWII warship in 1968, the living conditions sucked, and the workload was mentally and physically defeating for a non-rate.

Life wouldn't get any better for the rest of my deployment. Back home in the States, the 1968 election was right around the corner.

Chapter 7

Politics, War, and Arduous Life at Sea

Enemy Antiaircraft Weapons. North Vietnam used 57-mm (above), 85-mm (right), and 100-mm (below) weapons, as well as surface-to-air missiles (bottom) to combat U.S. aircraft in Laos.

Anti-aircraft systems North Vietnam used against US aircraft

Fall 1968

As described in chapter 1, Johnson was making progress with the Paris peace talks in fall 1968. The presidential race between Nixon and Humphrey was running tight. Little did we know at the time that the peace negotiations would soon fall apart, thanks to Nixon's secret treasonous acts in order to gain the presidency.

I certainly didn't know this was all happening at the time. I was floating off the coast of Vietnam in an old WWII aircraft carrier. I was working and sweating my ass off twenty hours a day in an environment where accidents were just waiting to happen. The ship and its crew were pushed to their limits, which only heightened the possibilities of shipboard accidents.

And for what? A self-centered, self-serving individual running for president who put his personal gain above those serving and fighting for their nation.

October 1, 1968
Dear Sandra,

The captain came over the 1MC yesterday and said that planes from the Hancock *are going to attack a North Vietnamese (NV) surface-to-air missile (SAM) site. This is a Russian-equipped missile site built and manned by the NV. The captain said this site has been responsible for downing several planes from other US carriers serving in the Gulf of Tonkin. The captain explained it's a risky mission for the pilots, but the site has to be destroyed.*

Also, the Hancock *will arrive back in the States in March and deploy again for Vietnam in July. Not much time to be together in the States.*

The captain just came over the 1MC and said our planes

were successful in blowing up the SAM site. He said NV didn't
even get a missile off at our planes.

October 2, 1968
Dear Sandra,
About two hours ago, we lost another plane—shot down.
They were unable to find the pilot.

Twenty miles northwest of Vinh, this A-4 jet was hit in the
wing by AAA fire. The commander (CDR) flew his burning
aircraft toward the sea and was unable to jettison his bombs.
As he crossed the coast, he ejected. But the aircraft
immediately blew up, either killing the CDR or knocking him
unconscious. He did not surface after parachuting into the
sea.

A small fishing boat retrieved his body. His remains were
finally handed over to the United States in March 1990.

October 3, 1968
Dear Sandra,
Lost another pilot today. The LT flying an F-8 jet crashed
his aircraft while returning to the carrier from a mission
over North Vietnam. The aircraft suffered a control failure,
pitched down into a dive, and hit the water right off the
starboard side of the ship, killing the LT.

October 5, 1968
Dear Sandra,
I spent all day working in the engine room rigging
temporary venting to move the heavy-oil vapor from above
the reduction gears. The ship has been operating at flank
speed (218 to 228 rpm) and dragging steam to 585 psi. The
lube oil in the reduction gears is very hot and producing a

*heavy-oil vapor. Sandra, remember how on the dependents'
day cruise you became sick from the fumes in the engine
room?*

In June 1968, prior to my first deployment, the captain
had hosted a dependents' day cruise. The ship pulled out for
an eight-hour cruise with dependents on board. This gave
dependents the opportunity to experience the operation of a
warship at sea and to see the duties their loved ones
performed at sea.

Sandra was pregnant with Heide, and it didn't take much
to upset her stomach. In particular, the oil fumes from the
reduction gears, along with other odors, were very strong at
times.

October 8, 1968

Dear Sandra,

*On our transit from Hawaii to the South China Sea, the
ship encountered bad weather. The sea was really rough.
Several fifty-five-gallon drums were washed overboard and
hit one of the ship's screws. The report is, it may be cracked.*

*The captain said the ship might have to enter dry dock in
Yokosuka, Japan, to repair the cracked screw. This will
happen after our final line commitment in the Gulf of Tonkin
but before returning to the States. Haven't heard if this will
extend the deployment or if the Pacific command will reduce
our line commitment.*

October 12, 1968

Dear Sandra,

*I borrowed eighteen bucks and bought you a jade ring at
the ship's store. I'm excited for you to see it.*

I received fresh apples Mom and Dad sent from the Apple

House in Lake City. This was a reason to smile!

A friend just walked into the compartment. He broke his hand in a car accident while on leave and had to remain stateside when the ship left for deployment. He was offered a different billet but requested to return to the Hancock. *The aft engine room has been short on staff, so his return will be a plus.*

First, the ring: I seldom borrowed money, but I saw this ring and was worried it would sell fast.

At the beginning of each month, the 3,200 men aboard the ship were paid in cash. Disbursing stations were set up alphabetically at various locations in the ship. You'd step up to a table with your military ID, and the distribution officer would look up your name, count out your pay, and hand you cash. I'd then go up to the post office and purchase a money order, sending all but twenty dollars home to Sandra. I didn't need a lot of money on the ship, and when the ship pulled into port, I usually stood by for other machinist's mates so I could make more money.

Second, the apples: Imagine having a fresh apple in your hand on a ship serving powdered shit for food. Imagine anticipating the first juicy, sweet bite. It was a moment in time for me.

I shared my apples with a couple of friends in the compartment. So now imagine three sailors eating fresh apples sitting on the deck in the berthing compartment, drifting for a short time with thoughts of enjoyment instead of the reality that life's a bitch aboard the ship.

Sandra and I travel most every fall to Lake City to purchase fresh apples, bringing back my memories of this moment.

October 13, 1968

Dear Sandra,

We leave Yankee Station tomorrow and head for the PIs. We should pull into Subic Bay on the seventeenth, then pull out and head for Singapore.

Sunday's chow was worse than shit. I went down to the ship's gedunk (snack bar) and bought a couple of cookies.

I just can't get a decent meal. The food has really been bad at the end of this line period. The mess cooks are back to serving powdered everything again. The worst is the powdered milk, which is made with warm water. There's no ice, and the drinking water temperature is above ninety degrees. Any ice produced in the enlisted galley goes to the officers' galley.

I developed a taste for warm tomato juice while on my first cruise. It was served at room temperature and tasted better than the powdered milk or Kool-Aid made with ninety-degree water from the ship's evaporators. I still drink warm tomato juice today.

I remember how one of the non-rated machinist's mates from the aft engine room was temporary assigned duty (TAD) to the mess hall for three months. I walked past him once on the mess deck. He had a long wooden paddle and was stirring liquid in a big vat.

"What are you doing?" I asked him.

"I'm making Kool-Aid for the officers' mess," he said. "I'll add a little favor to it."

He then picked up a dirty floor mop from the corner and used it to stir the officers' Kool-Aid with this asshole grin on his face. I can still see his expression. This sailor, a friend, was a little deranged—seriously.

I removed myself ASAP, not wanting to be a part of that joke if he got caught.

October 21, 1968

Dear Sandra,

I lit off and brought the Number 4 generator online. I'm scheduled to light off the Number 3 generator at 0000. The generators are located in the boiler rooms, where the temperature is around 140 degrees—hot.

The *Hancock* had four turbo-steam-driven generators that each produced 1250 kilowatts (kW) and two emergency diesel generators that each produced 500 kW. M Division personnel were responsible for the operation, repair, and maintenance of the steam turbines driving the electrical generators as well as the auxiliary support equipment. E Division personnel were responsible for the generator and the electrical panel board. Operation of the mechanical and electrical systems was shared by a machinist's mate and an electrician's mate. These two sailors controlled one-fourth of the electrical current serving the ship.

As a machinist's mate lighting off the generator, I would start the auxiliary system and wait for a twenty-eight-inch vacuum, then I would open the throttle valve, introducing 600 psi of auxiliary steam to the turbine. The whine of the steam turbine coming up to speed was always a thrill. Maybe the turbine didn't smoke black like Uncle Ray's diesel tractor going up the long winding hill, but it was still horsepower you could feel at your fingertips. Powering up the steam turbine never got old and was always an adrenaline rush.

Once the steam turbine was up to speed and all my systems were functioning properly, I'd give the electrician a thumbs-up. It was very noisy in the boiler room, making verbal communication difficult even from a short distance.

The electrician was responsible for synchronizing his generator with the ship's other three generators. This was a manual process—a very delicate and touchy operation. If the process were not conducted with precise timing, the generator and turbine could be damaged. It could possibly knock the other generators offline, and the ship could lose all electrical power.

Once the Number 3 generator synchronized with the other generators, the electrician would start adding electrical load to the generator. The mechanical governor on the steam turbine would continue to open the steam valve to maintain the required rpm. The high-pitched whine of the steam turbine would become louder and more pronounced as the electrical load was added.

My eyes had to be focused on the gauge panel, ensuring that all mechanical systems continued to operate properly. Knowledge and attention to detail was critical to ensure that human error and/or mechanical failure did not occur, as these would threaten all those in the boiler room and the mission of the ship.

October 23, 1968

Dear Sandra,

The ship is heading toward the equator and will cross it tomorrow, en route to Singapore.

Crossing the equator is an ageless mariners' tradition with initiation rituals. You cross the equator as "pollywog" and go through an initiation to become a "shellback." The rituals were humorous for those who were already shellbacks and nightmarish for those who weren't.

Initiation on the *Hancock* was an all-day event, and most

everyone participated. Any pollywogs who elected not to participate had to report to a designated compartment and remain there all day. If you agreed to participate, you had to wear a white T-shirt and roll your right pant leg above the knee, identifying you as a pollywog. You became fair game for harassment and abuse.

Harassment meant being led to the chow hall to be fed lima beans that looked, smelled, and tasted like green shit. The abuse consisted of being hit in the ass with a two-foot fire hose if you didn't do exactly as a shellback required of you.

The final part of the initiation took place on the flight deck. Numerous nasty events required your participation. Again, you were beat on your ass with the fire hose if you resisted a shellback's request and/or if your performance of a request was substandard. You might also be put in a stockade and treated to additional abuse until you acquiesced.

One the events on the flight deck included having to crawl on your hands and knees up to the "fat baby" and kiss his belly button. The fat baby was the fattest sailor on the ship, and he was wearing nothing but soggy, smelly undertrunks.

As you crawled up between the fat baby's legs, you'd have to stop, look up at him, and say, "My I kiss your belly button?" He'd then take a handful of garbage and slap it on his fat belly. And as you placed your lips close to his fat, hairy, ugly belly, he'd grab your head, push it into his belly, and rub it around several times. It was humiliating!

After kissing the fat baby's belly, you were required to crawl through a garbage chute. This was a long, round canvas chute filled with garbage from the chow hall. You know, like the food they served daily! It was bad and slimy, and it stunk like puke.

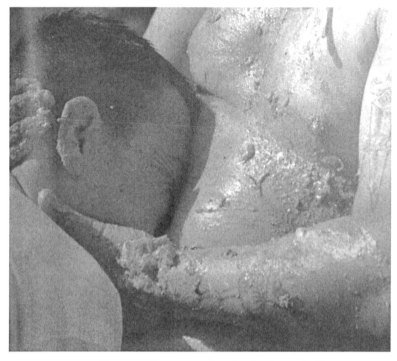

Pollywog kissing the fat baby's belly

Upon exiting the chute, you'd climb onto the platform of a huge tank filled with water. You had to jump into the tank and wash off the garbage clinging to your body. More accurately, a shellback would hit you in the ass with a fire hose filled with sand, knocking you into the tank.

October 25, 1968
Dear Sandra,

The ship pulled into Singapore. Electrical power is 50 cycle on shore while it's 60 cycle on the Hancock. *So, we have to run two generators in port, which is extra work for the machinist's mate.*

My plans are to catch up on sleep and study for my military requirements test. I did leave the ship to find some decent food. There was a food truck serving fish-and-chips. Finally, some good food.

The captain has informed the crew that our next line period will be thirty-five days. M Division is short on machinist's mates, so I'll be standing four on, four off, plus I'll be assigned to working parties bringing aboard food and bombs. I'm expecting the conditions for the next line period to be very taxing.

I remember walking off the gangplank and seeing several food trucks lined up on the dock to serve the *Hancock* and several British ships moored nearby. As a Scandinavian, I grew up eating meatballs and potatoes. I hadn't heard of fish-and-chips, but the deep-fried odor coming from that food truck pulled me in. The batter-fried fish and french fries were absolutely outstanding!

October 31, 1968

Dear Sandra,

We pulled out of Singapore. I'm standing watch on Number 3 throttle. The ship is heading back to Yankee Station.

In the hopes of restarting the Paris peace talks, President Johnson announced the end of Operation Rolling Thunder on this day. It was a complete halt of US bombing on North Vietnam, north of the twentieth parallel. But as we now know, Nixon, the self-chosen one (my words), undermined those hopes.

November 1, 1968

Dear Sandra,

I worked with my second-class machinist's mate conducting scheduled tests on the Number 3 generator. Then we secured and pumped oil out of its sump, then refilled it. I didn't hit my rack until 0130, and then I was called for watch at 0345. Less than two hours of sleep.

November 4, 1968

Dear Sandra,

I'm studying hard for the MM3 military requirements test, which I'm taking tomorrow. However, finding time to study is difficult.

November 6, 1968

Dear Sandra,

I'm standing generator watch, four hours on and four hours off for the next month. This is going to be a long, hot, and miserable line period. During the last line period, the Hancock flew sorties and dropped 300,000 pounds of bombs on the enemy. With three aircraft carriers on the line, that's about 1 million pounds of bombs per month—and we can't win the war!

November 9, 1968

Dear Sandra,

Just got back from the chow hall. The food was terrible. Haven't been able to eat that shit since we left Singapore. The ship must not have brought aboard fresh chow when we were in Singapore.

November 11, 1968

Dear Sandra,

Good news! I was told today I passed the military requirements test. I can take the professional exam for third-class machinist's mate in February.

November 15, 1968

Dear Sandra,

There was a 600-psi auxiliary steam leak on the Number 3 generator. My second class and I changed a 600-psi steam flex flange. It was a lot of sweat and hard work. Again, the boiler room is 140 degrees, and we weren't working under a fresh-air blower. We were soaked with sweat, and asbestos insulation was clinging to our clothes. The thick metal flanges and the one-inch bolts were extremely hot. It was a knuckle-busting job. It all made for miserable working conditions.

November 16, 1968

Dear Sandra,

A plane crashed on the flight deck late last night. The pilot came in too low and hit the rounddown on the back of the ship. As soon as the pilot felt the plane crash, he ejected. The plane exploded. Then the plane crashed into another plane on the flight deck, starting a huge fire and causing havoc.

When the pilot punched out of his disabled plane, he parachuted down but got caught on the wire safety netting on the bow of the ship. Landing in the very front of the bow, he broke both feet. If he had landed in the sea in front of the ship, he most likely would have been sucked under the ship and killed by the four large screws.

I remember this incident, as I was standing watch on the Number 3 generator when it happened. I was standing under the fresh-air blower when all of a sudden, heavy smoke started coming out of it. Not knowing a plane had crashed on the flight deck, I became very concerned, as the Number 3 boiler room was filling with smoke. The captain sounded general quarters to establish control of the havoc on the flight deck. In a few minutes, the smoke diminished and general quarters was secured. I later found out about the crash.

F-8 pilot ejecting after crash-landing on a carrier. Now visualize this type of crash at night, in the dark.

In 2016, I attended a veterans' rally at my granddaughter's school, and I met a veteran who had served on the USS *Hancock* as an airdale during my first cruise. As we talked, he gave me further details about this incident.

He said that because the accident happened late at night, it was hard to see the pilot parachuting down. To those on the flight deck, it appeared that the pilot had gone into the ocean. Hours later, the next morning, he was found hanging from the metal netting on the bow. The good news: he didn't end up lost at sea. The bad news: he hung there on the bow for many hours in the dark of night with two broken feet.

November 17, 1968

Dear Sandra,

The first class and second class tested me on training and casualty control generator drills last night. I made no mistakes. I'm confident in my training and knowledge. These types of drills are challenging but exciting.

Also, I found out Nixon was elected president. Sure hope he has a better game plan for the war than President Johnson had.

Starting in November 1968, Task Force Seventy-Seven concentrated on Operation Commando Hunt, a covert aerial interdiction campaign with the air force. Also beginning in November, the military brought massive airpower to bear against the Ho Chi Minh Trail, destroying thousands of trucks.

I can attest to the destruction of trucks. The television in the berthing compartment provided a daily update of flight operations. We saw video of trucks getting blown up. In some cases, the trucks were hidden under the jungle canopy, but US radar was still able to target them.

Operation Commando Hunt slowed the flow of supplies on the Ho Chi Minh Trail. Ultimately, though, it was considered another failure.

November 18, 1968

Dear Sandra,

I received a letter from you postmarked November 2, 1968. Sixteen days to receive a letter—and you paid airmail rate!

November 19, 1968

Dear Sandra,

Major problems today. The boiler technicians (BTs) found black oil in the feed water! Black oil is baked and caked in the steam drums of the Number 5, 6, 7, and 8 boilers. It's one and a half inches thick!

The engineering department secured the Number 3 and 4 boiler rooms, the Number 3 and 4 generators, and the aft engine room. The ship is operating on only two steam generators and two main engines (Number 1 and 2), which means only two screws.

The forward engine room is operating at max rpm on the Number 1 and 2 main engines. They're trying to reach as much speed as possible to launch jet aircraft so we can continue the scheduled bombing operations.

They're estimating it'll take eight days to clean the caked black oil out of the steam drums. That's going to be a very hot and dirty job. Being a boiler technician is one of the worst, if not *the worst job, on the ship. This equipment breakdown reduces the ship's maximum speed to 15 knots, increases the danger when launching aircraft, and adds to the complexity of completing the ship's mission.*

The Number 5, 6, 7, and 8 boilers were shut down, and work immediately began to dismantle the extremely hot boilers and open both the watersides and firesides. These boilers had been operating at 850 degrees, making the repair process a nightmare for the BTs. After a short cooldown period for the opened boilers, the BTs crawled into the watersides to "punch tubes." Using an air-operated high-speed brush, they had to ream each tube clean. There were hundreds of tubes. The BTs would come out of the boilers drenched in sweat and covered with black soot. It was a god-awful job!

November 23, 1968
Dear Sandra,

The BTs lit off the Number 5 and 6 boilers, and the aft engine room is steaming on two boilers. However, the BTs found salt in the feed water and had to secure the Number 6 boiler to correct this mechanical failure and flush the system. The aft engine room is now steaming on one boiler supplying the Number 2 main engine. The Number 3 main engine is shut down. The word is, the old man (the captain) is pissed, so the heat is on.

November 24, 1968: Thanksgiving Day
Dear Sandra,

The captain announced holiday routine, and the mess cooks are cooking steaks on the flight deck. There's a boxing match on the hanger bay. However, the ship never stops at sea, so no rest for the engine room crew. I didn't get up to the flight deck for a steak. Hate to be ungrateful, but usually the steak from overseas is tasteless and full of gristle.

November 25, 1968
Dear Sandra,

The singing group the Cascades flew aboard to perform for the crew on the hanger deck. Missed it. I was standing generator watch.

November 26, 1968
Dear Sandra,

The ship is heading for Japan. Our line commitment was shortened due to the problems in the boiler rooms. The captain said the temperature will be a high of forty-five and a low of twenty degrees when we reach Japan. This will be great for the engine rooms. They won't be so hot.

The engine rooms did cool down and were reasonably comfortable. Also, the cooler seawater temperature meant the main engines could reach a vacuum of twenty-eight and a half inches. This improved the main engines' performance and took a little stress off the top watch and his crew in the engine room.

November 27, 1968
Dear Sandra,

The Hancock *came too close when pulling alongside the supply ship USS* Camden. *Our elevator collided with the* Camden. *Also, the* Camden's *refueling lines caught one of our F-8 jets and dragged it into a carrier onboard delivery (COD) plane. Both planes were dragged over the side of the* Hancock *and fell onto the supply ship. Her deck was filled with twelve hundred 250-pound bombs ready to be off-loaded to the* Hancock. *Also, the F-8 had air-to-air missiles attached under her wings and a "plane captain" sitting in it.*

Nobody was hurt on either ship, but this was a very intense and very dangerous situation.

F-8 jet and a COD plane lie on the USS Camden. *This accident could have developed into a major disaster for both ships.*

The USS *Camden* was a newer supply ship, commissioned in 1967. It could replenish carriers or other ships with ammo, fuel, and commissary. In comparison, the older supply ships provided only a single replenishment. This meant replenishments every third day instead of every day.

My research includes information about the incident from a chief petty officer who was an eyewitness aboard the USS *Hancock.* He described how the *Camden*'s jet fuel and black oil lines tore apart and drenched both the *Hancock* and the *Camden* with flammable fuel. In the photo, note the oil stains on the side of the *Camden.*

The jet fuel could have ignited on the supply ship—with its deck loaded with twelve hundred bombs. Or if even one of those bombs had exploded as the planes landed on the *Camden*, all the other bombs would have exploded in a chain reaction. Or the air-to-air missile attached to the F-8 jet could have exploded or launched.

In other words, this incident could have turned deadly. The ifs are numerous. Both ships dodged a major disaster. Both ships could have sunk. There's no doubt in my mind, the *Hancock* dodged a catastrophe.

Here are my thoughts as to who was at fault for this accident. I'm going to get a little technical, but hang with me.

As I stated in my November 23 letter to Sandra, the aft engine room was operating Number 2 and 3 main engines with only the Number 5 and 6 boilers. Boilers Number 7 and 8 were still out of commission. Then salt water was found in the Number 6 boiler, and it was secured (stopped), as was the Number 3 main engine. This meant the ship was dragging the Number 3 screw and operating the Number 2 main engine with steam supplied only from the Number 5 boiler. This limited the Number 2 main engine's horsepower by 50 percent.

With only three screws operational and the fourth screw dragging, it would be very challenging for the captain to maintain control and precise movement of the *Hancock* as she pulled alongside the *Camden* to match her exact speed. And if needed, an emergency breakaway would be dangerous without proportional thrust available from all four screws.

The captain of the *Hancock* was maneuvering the aircraft carrier to pull alongside the *Camden* as she maintained a constant speed. The Number 1 (starboard) and 4 (port) main engines and screws were available to develop maximum horsepower and thrust. However, the Number 2 (starboard) main engine and screw could only develop at 50 percent of maximum, and the Number 3 (port) main engine was not operational, and the screw was dragging.

The unequal thrust from the three operational screws and the dragging fourth screw created abnormal rudder compensation while pulling along the port side of the *Camden*. It challenged the helmsmen, as the *Hancock*'s bow could drift to his starboard, toward the *Camden*. The helmsman's routine rudder operation became everything but routine.

Nearing alongside the *Camden*, the captain had to slow the forward movement of the *Hancock* and ordered astern throttle to match the *Camden*'s exact speed. When pulling alongside a supply ship with all four main engines operating, the captain's normal operational sequence would be to order (via telegraph to the throttle watch) all engines to stop, then order all engines astern throttle one-third in order to slow forward movement. With equal thrust from all four screws, this operational event would keep the ship parallel to the supply ship as astern thrust slowed the ship's forward movement to match the speed of the supply ship. I performed this sequence many times while standing throttle watch in the aft engine room. I can attest to the constant throttle and rpm changes from the captain on the bridge to maneuver the *Hancock*'s equal thrust. Once we were alongside, the bridge ordered minor rpm changes of only one or two rpms at a time. These rpm changes were constantly issued from the bridge in order to keep the ship at the same exact speed and aligned with the supply ship. The throttle watch was so busy making throttle changes that a second throttle watch was added just to record the rpm changes ordered by the bridge.

But in this situation, the astern operation ordered by the captain caused the *Hancock* to drift close to the *Camden*. So, the captain next ordered an emergency breakaway to avoid a collision.

The question is, did the captain realize—before he made the order—that the astern operation and the unequal thrust of each screw would cause the ship to drift? It's impossible to know what he was thinking in that moment.

But I believe he did understand what was happening once he noticed the ship was not responding favorably to astern operation. In a matter of seconds, he must have mentally reviewed years of past experience and training to decide how to avoid a collision. I think he knew, then, that the uneven thrust from the ship's screws was causing the ship's abnormal response.

I also think he was aware that an emergency breakaway could be perilous, due to the unequal thrust from each screw. But he had no other choice. He had to give the order for an emergency breakaway.

With a dragging screw and unequal thrust from the remaining screws, the *Hancock* drifted to starboard and toward the *Camden*. The ships collided!

We all have our oh-shit moments, and this was an oh-shit moment for the captain!

Main engine throttle station and telegraph from bridge

With all the major problems the *Hancock* experienced on my first deployment, I thought Captain Greer would be held responsible for the collision with the *Camden*. However, Captain Greer went on to achieve the rank of four-star admiral before retiring in 1976.

I was interested in what the officer of the bridge logged about this incident, at least to verify my theory. The ship's logs from the bridge would verify by number the main engines and boilers operating at the time of this collision with the USS *Camden*. However, these logs were missing, and I was unable to locate them.

Chapter 8

The Final Months of My First Deployment

North Korea captured the USS Pueblo in January 1968, yet US leaders did nothing until the end of the year.

Engineering problems had crippled the *Hancock.* Operating with only three screws and 60 percent horsepower, her maximum speed was now only 18 knots. Unable to obtain the speed required to launch continuous air strikes over Vietnam, the ship's mission was redirected to the waters of South Korea to serve as a show of "strength" against North Korea.

November 28, 1968

Dear Sandra,

One of the men in M Division's father passed away, and the M Division officer won't allow him to fly home for the funeral.

The Number 4 boiler room won't be operational for quite a while. They found holes in the superheater. Also, the Number 3 main engine developed a dangerous steam leak. A 600-psi superheated steam leak can injure or be lethal to a sailor. The top watch heard a whistle-like noise.

We're operating main engines Number 1, 2, and 4 at flank speed, pulling steam pressure to 585 psi during flight operation to maintain as much air as possible across the flight deck for launching aircraft.

The boiler technicians (BTs) have to replace the tubes in the Number 7 and 8 boilers. Replacing the tubes means taking all the fire brick out of each boiler, which is a huge job—very hot and dirty. The BTs are sweating their asses off. A friend I met in boot camp is assigned to the Number 4 boiler room, and he suffered third-degree burns while removing the fire brick in the Number 7 boiler.

November 29, 1968

Dear Sandra,

I'm so tired I can't think straight! The ship is heading toward Japan.

December 1, 1968

Dear Sandra,

I don't have much time to write. I went two days with only five hours of sleep.

December 3, 1968

As mentioned earlier in the book, North Korea had hijacked the communications ship USS *Pueblo* and its crew in January 1968. So what did Johnson do to show his resolve and to pressure North Korea to release our prisoners?

He wimped out. Eleven months later, he sent the *Hancock* to South Korean waters so South Korean dignitaries could be flown aboard for an air show. That was Johnson's pathetic attempt to say, "Don't mess with the US!" Really, this wasn't even good window dressing. What a bunch of bullshit.

Compare that to Johnson's response in 1964, when North Vietnam attacked the USS *Maddox*. He called it "open aggression on the high seas" and used it to launch the Vietnam War. But when the *Pueblo* was captured, all Johnson and his cronies did was send a broken-down WWII ship that had been limping along at sea after colliding with another ship and, by the grace of God, had barely avoided a major disaster.

I and the other sailors were working long hours, literally sweating our asses off, and eating shit for food. And now we were supposed to stage an air show for the South Korean government with the intent that it might scare North Korea into acquiescing to our military power? What a joke!

When the North Korean leader opened the newspaper the

next morning and saw the South Korean prime minister seated next to the admiral of Task Force Seventy-Seven aboard the *Hancock*, he probably fell off his chair laughing. North Korea knew Johnson was weak when he didn't immediately retaliate after the *Pueblo* was captured.

USS Hancock *air show with Rear Admiral Morrison (left), Prime Minister Chung Il Kwom (center), and Admiral Bringle (right)*

December 5, 1968
Dear Sandra,
The ship is pulling into Sasebo, Japan. I hope to catch up on sleep and study for my third-class professional test.

December 6, 1968
Dear Sandra,
Today I had a glass of fresh, cold milk. It tasted so good!

This was the first glass of fresh milk I've had since leaving the States. Hopefully the ship's enlisted crew will get some good food.

Thinking back, there's no way the ship's officers were being fed the same slop the enlisted men were eating!

December 7, 1968
Dear Sandra,
  The navy has hired Japanese women as yardbirds to clean the "voids" below the Number 4 boiler room. Different, but better them than me. It's a dark, dirty, and nasty job. They came down to the Number 4 boiler room, stripped down to nothing, put on only a pair of coveralls, and didn't worry if sailors were watching them change.

These women were taking any job possible to feed their families. I also remember walking down the streets of Japan and seeing a little old lady (she looked old to me) operating a jackhammer on a street under construction. Really sad.

December 9, 1968
Dear Sandra,
  I'm working on my machinist's mate third class (MM3) professional courses and have completed four of the six courses. It looks like I can take the test in February. I'm trying to find time to study.
  The word is, there will be no combat pay for the month of December. The ship needs to be on the line (on Yankee Station) for six days. Also, we're heading to Hong Kong and should set anchor on the fourteenth.

December 14, 1968

Dear Sandra,

The ship is anchored off the coast of Hong Kong. Sailors are not allowed to take American currency to shore. Before leaving the ship on liberty, we have to exchange US currency for "funny money" if we want to purchase items in Hong Kong.

Hong Kong was under British control in the 1960s. Today, it's under Chinese control. In 1968, the United States was concerned that China would intercept our currency and disrupt our currency flow.

Hong Kong was a free port, and sailors could buy custom-made tailored suits and custom-made shoes very cheaply. Later, on my second cruise, I had clothes tailored.

When the ship was anchored in the harbor, sampans—flat-bottomed boats—would pull alongside the ship and collect all the garbage. Those staffing the sampans would sort through the garbage and separate out the food for consumption or sale. I considered the food garbage; they considered it a lifeline.

Mid-December 1968

I sent Sandra the midcruise issue of the Hancock *Signature*, a magazine put out by the Armed Forces Press Service. This issue of the *Signature* informed the sailors' families and loved ones about the activity during the first four months of deployment. Sandra saved the issue I sent her.

As I read an article Captain Greer wrote fifty years ago, I started thinking, *He didn't tell the entire story.* So here's his story versus mine. What you're about to read is very important, and I ask that you read it twice. And as you are reading and rereading, think about the title of the book and how my story parallels with that of the captain of the USS *Hancock.*

Here are quotes from Captain Greer:

- **"Commencing the cruise with inadequate training under our belts"**
  - As I read that quote fifty years later, I'm thinking, *The Hancock and the crew were deployed to a war zone, even though they knew we were inadequately trained? Unbelievable!* It is inexcusable that the president, the Joint Chiefs of Staff, and the commander of the Pacific fleet sent a naval ship into combat with an inadequately trained crew.
  - In naval books such as *American Boys,* the ships' captains state the same problems: their crews were inadequately trained and their ships' engineering systems were in disrepair and unfit for engagement of warfare—yet they were ordered to deploy. I shake my head today with disgust.

- **"We suffered some predictable casualties"**
  - My question today: Were the predictable casualties due to inadequate training and/or equipment failure?

- **"Equipment reliability had not been assured"**
  - You have to read between the lines with this quote. What it means is, "Equipment failure was foreseeable." I presume the ship's engineering officer had notified the captain of his concerns about the engineering systems

prior to deployment. And I'm sure the captain expressed these concerns to the Seventh Fleet admiral. However, the higher up the chain of command the information was relayed, the less consideration it was given. So, a ship with unreliable mechanical and electrical systems was deployed to a war zone.

- **"We were plagued with personnel shortages in total numbers and in critical talent"**
  - o This quote explains why I'd been complaining to Sandra about M Division working the living shit out of me and allowing me very little sleep for the last four months. Captain Greer was saying the ship was understaffed when it was ordered to deploy. Not only understaffed but lacking critical talent. Meaning, the *Hancock* lacked personnel with the seasoned knowledge to operate, maintain, and repair the ship's systems and equipment.
  - o To summarize, the captain stated that we were "commencing the cruise." Understand, this wasn't a "cruise"—the ship was "deployed" to a war zone! In fact, it was deployed to a war zone despite having personnel shortages, inadequately trained personnel who lacked critical talent, and unreliable mechanical and electrical systems. And worst of all, we were facing "predictable causalities." The ship was a disaster waiting to happen.
  - o The above problems weren't isolated to just the *Hancock*. Many ships in the Seventh Fleet experienced the same problems. These

problems were known up the chain of command of both the Seventh Fleet and the Pacific fleet. Yet the chain of command turned a blind eye. And for that, America's youth suffered.

o   As detailed in *American Boys*, the USS *Frank E. Evans* also had inadequate training and substandard equipment and systems. And seventy-four sailors lost their lives when she was cut in half by another ship. I'll discus this disaster later in the book.

Now here's my story. Here's what the captain's article *didn't* say and what he failed to communicate to the families and loves ones:

- The ship's evaporators broke down several times. Water hours were established, making life miserable for the sailors.
- The Number 2 engine room, the Number 3 and 4 boiler rooms, and the Number 3 and 4 generators were out of commission for four days, requiring major repairs at sea and pushing the crew beyond expectation. These repairs entailed around-the-clock sweat and toil in extreme conditions. The ship was now steaming with only two main engines.
- The *Hancock* collided with the *Camden*. As discussed in chapter 7, it could have been a major disaster for both ships.
- An emergency in the aft engine room resulted in Mr. Schmuck, a chief warrant officer, unknowingly almost backing the *Hancock* into a destroyer

escort.
- There was an electrical switchboard fire in the aft engine room, it blew up, and those standing watch were subjected to 160-degree heat as the ship continued to fly air strikes against the enemy.

The United States government did not have a strategy to win the Vietnam War. It deployed an old WWII aircraft carrier to the war zone even though the ship was short on personnel and critical talent, even though the crew was inadequately trained, and even though the equipment and systems were unreliable. And because of it, we suffered "predicable casualties." These facts come straight from the words of Captain Greer. This is unforgiveable and forever a stain on the United States!

December 20, 1968
Dear Sandra,
The ship is pulling out of Hong Kong today. I'm standing six hours on, six hours off on generators. M Division is still short on qualified personnel to cover the generators.

This only proves the points made above. Standing six hours on and six hours off was brutal duty due to the excessive heat and noise in the boiler rooms.

Here's an example of a twenty-four-hour period when standing six on, six off: I'd wake at 2330 and then take over the generator watch at 2345. I'd make my way to the Number 3 boiler room. When I'd open the door to the 140-degree boiler room, it would be like walking into a blast furnace. I would descend down a steep ladder and proceed to the generator, walking between the Number 5 and Number 6 boilers on the upper level of the boiler room. I would then greet the boiler checkman, who was responsible for maintaining the water level in the boiler. He never had a smile on his face.

When I'd reach the generator, the machinist's mate I was relieving would update me as to the mechanical operation of the turbine. We'd stand face-to-face, yet we'd have to yell just to overcome the excessive noise in the boiler room.

While on duty, I'd stand under a fresh-air blower (90-plus-degree air) while watching the gauge panel on the generator for possible problems. There was no chair or place to sit down; it wasn't allowed. For the entire six hours, I had to stand on the metal deck plates, which cooked my feet. With one hand, I'd hang on to the short rope tied to the fresh-air duct's outlet grill. It'd take some weight off my legs, one at a time.

It was a noisy, hot, mundane six-hour watch, but I had to stay alert. The scream of the force-draft blowers serving the boilers and the high-pitch screech of the generator affected my hearing, even after I left the boiler room.

I'd be relieved from watch at 0545. I'd go up to the chow hall and look for something worth eating. I'd then go up to the berthing compartment around 0600 and catch a little sleep until 0730, at which time I'd muster in the aft engine room. I'd be assigned to repair and maintain machinery. I'd be allowed to eat at 1100, but I usually didn't eat anything. Instead, I'd hit my rack for forty minutes of sleep.

At 1130, the messenger would wake me to assume watch at 1145. I'd stand a six-hour watch from 1145 to 1545. I'd then grab a bite to eat, shit, shower, shave, and hit my rack for some much-needed sleep—only to be woken again at 2330 to repeat the past twenty-four hours. But more often than not, I'd get only three hours of sleep. As a non-rate, I'd be assigned to a three-hour working party. Or if there was equipment failure, I'd be called to help repair.

This would be my life for thirty days while the ship was deployed in the combat zone, flying airstrikes against the enemy or in transit to and from port.

December 23, 1968

North Korea finally released the American prisoners captured during the USS *Pueblo* incident. The POWs were severely beaten, starved, and mentally abused, yet the United States agreed to North Korea's terms of release. And then upon the POWs' arrival home, the navy admirals threw the *Pueblo* captain under the bus, blaming him for its capture. This is another a joke!

Bottom line: the United States military ordered a communications ship—with highly classified equipment, top-secret data, only one .50-caliber machine gun for defense, and no air or sea protection—to go into a chaotic Communist region where the United States had more foes than friends. Yet the navy admirals did not have the foresight to predict this level of aggression and/or a need to provide protection for this spy ship. Give me a break!

These admirals I refer to were highly educated, having graduated either from the best colleges or from the Annapolis naval academy. They had years of experience and were highly seasoned in military operations and procedures. To make an egregious error of this caliber is a dereliction of duty. *They* should have been court-martialed—not the captain of the *Pueblo*.

Understand, enlisted petty officers had been court-martialed for much less, such as for missing ships' movement. Busted to the rank of non-rate and thrown in the ship's brig, these sailors were used as examples to send a zero-tolerance message to other enlisted. Yet no discipline or charges were brought against the navy admirals responsible for North Korea's capture of a naval vessel and the imprisonment of eighty sailors. Unbelievable!

Fortunately, one civilian leader had his head screwed on straight. That was Clark Clifford, the secretary of defense. He said the prisoners had suffered enough and that no charges would be filed against the ship's captain or the crew. The entire incident was quietly swept under the rug.

December 24, 1968
Dear Sandra,

I've received no word on the birth of our baby yet. It's all that's on my mind.

I'll spend Christmas Eve standing watch on the Number 3 generator. The Bob Hope Show *came aboard and will perform at 2100 on the hanger deck. I'm scheduled for 1800 to 0000 generator watch, though, so I'll miss the big show.*

December 25, 1968
Dear Sandra,

This is our second Christmas away from each other. It only gets harder—missing you!

Christmas chow should be worth eating, so I'm looking forward to good food. I'm so tired, losing weight, and can't wait to return home to your cooking.

December 27, 1968
Dear Sandra,

The ship's chaplain called me to his office and told me I was the father of a healthy baby girl, born after midnight on the twenty-sixth. He said you're doing fine. He then read the telegram received by the ship.

Floating on the open sea ten thousand miles from home, I was extremely excited and happy when the chaplain read the telegram informing me I was the father of a baby girl, born at 12:06 a.m. on December 26, 1968. However, I was in a daze. Mentally, I couldn't visualize the hospital setting or Sandra and the baby.

The first photo I received of Sandra and Heide

I received this picture via mail a month later. To this day, I have no words to express my feelings upon seeing this first image of Sandra and our baby. Honestly, it brought quiet tears of joy to my eyes.

One thing I wish is that I would have asked the chaplain if I could have the telegram.

December 30, 1968
Dear Sandra,

The captain informed the crew that a plane carrying three thousand pounds of mail crashed—no mail.

The ship is on the line until February 9, then the ship is sailing to the PIs for one day and then to Yokosuka, Japan, for repairs. We'll then return to the States, arriving March 3.

January 1, 1969—New Year's Day
Dear Sandra,

Sandra, I found out some very good news today! The first class told me that the M Division officer chose two firemen to fly back to the States one month ahead of the ship, and they chose me because of my outstanding performance during the deployment. I don't have the exact date, but I'll let you know when I have additional details. I'll fly off the ship to Da Nang, then to the PIs, and then stateside.

January 2, 1969
Dear Sandra,

M Division was thinking about flying me off the ship on February 2, but I'm scheduled to take the E-4 machinist mate's test on the fourth. They want me to take the test before I fly off, so I'll fly on the sixth instead.

January 8, 1969
Dear Sandra,

The M Division senior officer—not Mr. Schmuck— approached me today and asked me what I thought of flying back to the States thirty days early. I told him I was delighted and thanked him. He then told me why I was picked. He said it was because of my outstanding performance during the cruise. They noticed! I not only worked my ass off but

174 ◆ Vietnam 1967–1971

sweated my ass off. I think I'm down to 145 pounds. I left boot camp at 165.

For the division officer to approach me, a non-rate, to express his appreciation and recognize my performance was a huge morale booster for me. It was rare to see the senior division officer and even rarer for him to speak to a non-rate.

I was the first fireman asked to help make repairs when needed. Why? Because they could depend on me. I was quick to learn and qualify for the various engine room watches, and I wasn't a slacker. My goal was to make second class petty officer and stand top watch in the aft engine room. The first class involved me as much as possible in operation, repairs, and maintenance to prepare me for future responsibilities. It's called on-the-job-training.

January 10, 1969
Dear Sandra,

The Hancock *has been extended on the line for a couple extra days because the aircraft carrier USS* Ranger *lost a main engine and is heading for the PIs for repair. Remember, earlier in the cruise, we lost two boiler rooms, two generators, and the aft engine room, yet we continued sea operations and the ship was deployed to South Korea. We didn't head in for repairs!*

January 11, 1969
Dear Sandra,

I'm standing generator watch in the Number 3 boiler room, and they have both the Number 5 and 6 boilers on the line. The ship is operating at flank speed during flight operation, and the boiler room is hot!

I'm counting the days until I fly off the ship on early leave.

January 13, 1969
Dear Sandra,

It's official: I fly off the ship to Da Nang on February 6. I take my test for E-4 on the fourth, and I'm studying hard. We need the money.

January 14, 1969
Dear Sandra,

The M Division officer signed my chit for the thirty-day leave to the States. The captain has given his word on letting us go—good news. As I said, I'll fly off the ship to Da Nang on February 6; then fly into Subic Bay, PIs; then take a sixty-mile bus ride through the PIs to Clark Air Base; then catch a military hop from Clark to Travis Air Force Base in California. I'm finally excited about something.

The XO (executive officer) said the ship will go into four-section duty when it returns to the States—good duty.

I have captain's inspection on the Number 3 generator tomorrow. I'm ready. The Number 3 generator has been meticulously cared for and its appearance says it all. I've painted "Mr. Clean" on the gauge panel.

January 15, 1968
Dear Sandra,

The captain never came down to the generator for inspection. I was disappointed. It was probably too hot, and he didn't want soot on his clothes. He probably doesn't like the smell of soot or burnt black oil either.

I still have a strong memory of descending down the ladder to the Number 3 boiler room to assume generator watch. I remember the smell of burnt Number 6 black oil, the small particles of soot in the air. I'm sure this is another reason why my lungs continue to lose capacity today. I never smoked, yet the capacity of my lungs decreases every year. My lungs are shot!

Not only was there the smell of burnt black oil and carbon from the boilers. There was also the very loud noise from the forced-air blowers and the feel of hot air as it hit your face. To enter a boiler room, you entered a small closure called an air lock. Shutting the first door then opening the second door of the air lock was difficult due to the negative pressure in the boiler room, which was created by the forced-air blowers providing air/oxygen to the boilers.

January 15, 1969

Dear Sandra,

I heard today the carrier USS Enterprise *has major problems and is returning to the States for repairs. This means the line period for one of the remaining three carriers will be extended. I don't think it'll be the* Hancock. *We've been deployed the longest.*

The nuclear aircraft carrier USS *Enterprise* was known as the Big E. On January 14, 1969, it was conducting operational-readiness drills seventy-five miles off the coast of Hawaii before steaming toward Vietnam for its fourth deployment. It was set to relieve the USS *Hancock*.

The *Enterprise*'s captain was turning to port to conduct flight operation when suddenly a Zuni rocket with a fifteen-pound warhead exploded under the wing of an F-4 Phantom parked on the stern. The exhaust from an MD-3A huffer, a tractor-mounted unit used to start aircraft, had inadvertently heated the rocket.

The explosion set off a series of chain reaction explosions. Several five-hundred-pound bombs ripped the ship open all the way to the waterline. Also, a six-thousand-gallon JP-5 jet fuel container was breached. The fuel ignited and poured down into the 03, 02, and 01 levels, and below the flight deck. The explosion also damaged the twin-agent firefighting units, which slowed the firefighting response.

After hours of death and destruction, the flight deck had an eighteen-by-twenty-two-foot hole, and twenty-eight sailors were killed, with another 314 injured. The *Enterprise* returned to Alameda under its own power for major repairs. Fifty-one days and $128 million later, the Big E set sail again for her fourth deployment to Vietnam.

As described in chapter 3, a Zuni rocket also set off the explosion causing fire, death, and destruction on the USS *Forrestal* in July 1967.

USS Enterprise *in serious distress*

As I look back, I'm reminded of how dangerous aircraft carriers were during the Vietnam War. And that danger was further augmented by the sailors' demanding workloads, long hours, high stress, breakdowns in morale, drug use, and lack of attention to detail. Reality is, the operation of a warship is a "team sport." But if someone drops the ball, it means losing more than a game. It can mean a disaster.

Keep in mind too, the lives lost on the USS *Enterprise* are not honored on the Vietnam Veterans Memorial (the Wall) nor counted toward the number of Vietnam War deaths. Because the *Enterprise* was en route to Vietnam when the disaster happened, these lives were technically not lost in the "combat zone." Therefore, they are not considered casualties of the war.

January 16, 1969
Dear Sandra,

The Hancock *pulled into the PIs today. I have more good news: due to the time difference, I leave the ship on February 6 yet will still make it home on February 6!*

January 17, 1969
Dear Sandra,

I went over to Grande Island for a few hours of R & R. I played baseball and horseshoes, and we were served free hot dogs, chips, and pop. Grande Island is a military recreation area, where personnel can enjoy time away from the ship without leaving the base. To get to the island, we boarded an old landing craft, like they used in WWII to deploy ground troops to enemy areas. On the front of the craft, the nose drops down to load and unload personnel and equipment. Different.

I boarded the battleship USS New Jersey. *She's docked*

not far from the Hancock. *The guns are massive, as is the armament. She can shoot a 2,700-pound armor-piercing shell twenty-three miles. She's stationed off the coast of Vietnam, providing support with her massive guns.*

January 20, 1969

This is the date Richard Nixon was inaugurated as the thirty-seventh US president. He campaigned on a pledge of "peace with honor." We didn't get either. Understand, that was just his campaign commitment to America, but his private pledge to South Vietnam was, "I'll give you a better outcome than Johnson."

Nixon's political ambitions took priority over his commitment to his military force—my words. Through the next four years of his presidency, he didn't focus on winning the war but rather on winning his reelection in 1972, which he did with a landslide vote.

After being sworn in as president, Nixon told the assembled crowd that the "government will listen. . . . Those who have been left out, we will try to bring in." But that same day, he obliterated his pledges of greater citizen control of government by signing National Security Decision Memorandum 2—a document that made sweeping changes to the national security power structure. Nixon's signature erased the influence that the State Department, the Department of Defense, and the CIA had over the Vietnam War and the course of the Cold War. The new structure put Nixon at the center, surrounded by loyal aids and a new national security director, Henry Kissinger. While previously serving in the Johnson administration, Kissinger had been the leak to the Nixon campaign, providing classified information about terms of the Paris peace talks.

The unprecedented creation of this secret extraconstitutional government undermined US policy and values. Ironically, Nixon sowed the seeds of his own destruction by creating a climate of secrecy, paranoia, and reprisal. He resigned from office in disgrace in 1974.

Nixon lost the war. Saigon fell to the North Vietnamese. The South Vietnamese suffered torture and death beyond imagination. The United States lost 58,000 military personnel, and thousands of veterans still suffer mentally and physically.

All for nothing.

Through my years of following politics, I've determined that the majority of politicians are two-faced, lying, self-serving sacks of shit. These are strong words, but a small amount of research confirms this opinion.

January 22, 1969

Dear Sandra,

I dropped my false teeth in the sink and broke off a tooth—another oh-shit moment. When I went up to the ship's dentist, he opened his drawer full of loose teeth, picked out one he thought would match, and glued it on. He didn't ask me what I thought of the color, how it looked, or if I liked it. He just glued it on and sent me on my way. It was probably a tooth he scavenged from a dead sailor's false plate.

A pipe broke in a void (the bowels of the ship), and I had to go down there to make the repairs. It's the hottest I've ever been. No electricity, no lights except a handheld battery-powered lantern, no ventilation. Dirty, dirty, dirty. I threw away my clothes.

As I think back, we should have had a canary down in the void so we would have known when the oxygen supply was low. Crawling into these voids, with no fresh air, wasn't smart. But you didn't question authority or repairs that needed to be made. It was "do as you're told."

January 25, 1969
Dear Sandra,

I worked eighteen hours straight making repairs. I'm so tired.

The navy has undercover investigators on the ship, trying to crack down on the drug use. I think a third of the ship is on bennies or dope of some kind.

Around this time, I received a letter from Sandra—it was actually the last letter from her during this deployment. She informed me that my friend Marvin, one of my groomsmen, had been drafted into the army. As I mentioned in chapter 5, the wedding was the last time I saw Marv alive. He died in Vietnam in late 1971.

But what I didn't mention in chapter 5 was how he died. Marv was a victim of fragging, a term used to describe the murder of an officer at the hands of a disgruntled US soldier. In particular, many of these murders were committed via a fragmentation grenade. In Marv's case, a disgruntled black soldier shot him in an NCOs (noncommissioned officers') club in November. He later died in December.

Marv was a great friend growing up in Farmington. His death is at the feet of President Nixon, who secretly extended the Vietnam War to ensure his reelection in 1971.

I ask that you please visit www.vvmf.org, the website for the Vietnam Veterans Memorial Fund. Go to the section titled "The Wall of Faces" and look up the entry for Marvin C. Briesacher. Read the story behind this killing and how the military swept it under the rug.

January 28, 1969

Dear Sandra,

I went up to sick bay to make sure my shots were up-to-date. The corpsman said I could pick up my shot card tomorrow. I need the shot card to travel internationally.

January 29, 1969

Dear Sandra,

The second class I report to received a Dear John letter from his wife. He's really down in the dumps. Also, he was chosen as M Division's second class to fly back to the States early. Now he has little to look forward to when returning to the States.

I picked up my shot card. It's a booklet listing all the shots I've received since entering the navy. I must look like a pincushion.

January 30, 1969

Dear Sandra,

I'm writing you this letter on watch at 2230 hours. Sandra, this is my last letter from this deployment. See you soon! Sounds good and feels even better. So, bye for now, and I'll be holding you in my arms soon!

February 3, 1969

It was our anniversary. We'd been married one year but had spent very little time together. I was looking forward to flying off the ship early and sharing time with Sandra again. It had been a very demanding deployment.

In the meantime, I was studying hard for my E-4 test on the fourth. Passing the test meant a pay increase of $100 per month. Also, E-4 petty officers were tasked with additional responsibilities, which eliminated many of the "shit jobs" in the engine room, such as polishing the brass, wire-brushing the deck plates, cleaning the bilges, chipping paint, and so on.

One example of a less-than-desirable job was inspecting the main engine's lube oil sump under the main reduction gear. The sump is essentially the oil pan for the carrier's main engine. The oil pan on your automobile holds six quarts of oil. An aircraft carrier's sump holds several hundred gallons of oil.

The first class called for the sump to be inspected for metal fragments. This procedure required you to strip down to only your underwear, and you were given one rag and a flashlight. You were then instructed to crawl through a small inspection hole and into the sump to look for metal fragments.

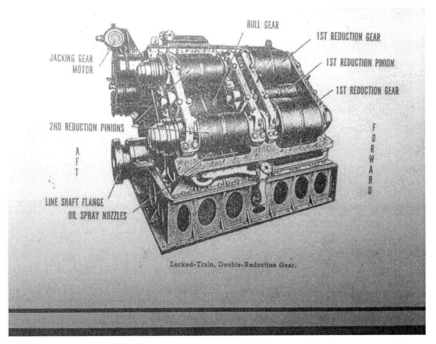

Note the six round inspection openings at the bottom of the reduction gears. The third from the right inspection cover was removed for access to the sump.

Once you were in the oil sump, there was absolutely no light. If you turned off your flashlight or if it malfunctioned, you couldn't see your fingers a quarter inch from your eyes. You had to be careful crawling on your belly as you worked your way through the baffles that kept the lube oil positioned as the ship rolled and pitched at sea.

After inspection, you'd crawl back out this very confined area. When you emerged, you had to have three items: your underwear, the rag, and the flashlight. This ensured that nothing was left in the oil sump. Of course, your body would be covered with lube oil. Not fun. If I remember, the lube oil was polychlorinated biphenyl (PCB) based. I mentioned this chemical back in chapter 4, and I'll discuss it later in the book again.

February 4, 1969

On the day I took my E-4 test, an LTJG flying an F-8 hit the rounddown on the back of the ship while landing. His jet veered to the left until it went overboard and crashed in the sea. The LTJG didn't eject, and his body was not recovered.

February 6, 1969

I packed my seabag and headed for the flight deck. The flight deck crew moved the C-2A aircraft, a carrier onboard delivery (COD) craft, onto the catapult, and the back door dropped down. I stood there watching as an air wing crew loaded a jet engine into the plane and secured it with bracing to the fuselage. Then they loaded nine aircraft carrier seats facing toward the back of the plane and secured those to the fuselage as well. All of this was completed in a very short period of time—seven to ten minutes.

The plane's crew chief motioned for nine of us sailors to board the plane and take a seat. He quickly instructed us on how to strap in and pull the straps as tight as we could—which I did. He then walked through the plane and pulled our straps even tighter.

I remember thinking, *Hope they have that engine secured.*

The door was shut and secured as the plane was readied for the catapult shot. The catapult released, and we were in the air—that quick. It's zero to 110 mph in two seconds and one hundred yards. I was instantly forced toward the back of the plane. Even though my straps had been retightened, there was slack as I felt my body pull from the seat. This was another first and a huge adrenaline rush!

COD launched from a carrier deck

In the Gulf of Tonkin on December 15, 1970, a C-2A COD was catapulted off the USS *Ranger*. Shortly after launch, it pitched up, stalled, and crashed into the sea. All sailors on board were killed. This occurred during my third deployment, when the *Hancock* was serving on Yankee Station in the Gulf of Tonkin with the USS *Ranger*.

Scuttlebutt was, they had a jet engine as cargo, and it broke loose from its bracing when the plane launched. It apparently slid to the back of the plane, causing the plane to pitch up and stall, falling backward into the ocean. Those sailors seated in the back of the plane were crushed, and the jet engine slid out of the back of the plane.

With internet research, I located the incident, date, and number of sailors killed, but there were no additional details other than what I've given above. During the Vietnam War, seven C-2A were lost or crashed.

After hearing about this crash with the COD from the *Ranger*, I'm glad the COD crew chief from the *Hancock* was mistake-free for my cat shot (catapult launch).

February 9, 1969

A few days after I left the *Hancock*, there was an aircraft accident leading to a loss of life. During night operations on Yankee Station, Lieutenant Commander (LCDR) Roger Meyers experienced a collapsed nose gear during a catapult launch in his A-4. His plane pitched down, crashed into the sea, and exploded. LCDR Meyers did not eject, and his body was not recovered.

Again, I urge you to visit "The Wall of Faces" and look for Roger Meyers's page to read the message his grandson wrote. As you read, please take pause and place yourself in the mind of this child. At the time of his grandfather's death, his mother was only a young child and his grandmother was the young widow of a fallen naval aviator. The loss of a husband, father, and grandfather caused pain and heartache for years to come.

Catapult bridle prepared for attachment to the nose gear of an A-4 Skyhawk

Imagine the knock on the door. Imagine how military personnel in full dress uniform notified this young wife that her husband had been killed in Vietnam. Imagine her young daughter standing by her side, clinging to her dress. Imagine as she heard there was no date and time to meet the arrival of the casket—the body was lost at sea.

Chapter 9

Stateside: 1969

Heide Jo, four months old

February 1969

On February 6, I was catapulted off the *Hancock* and flew to Da Nang. From there, I flew to Clark Air Base, to Travis Air Force Base, then to Minneapolis. Due to the change in time zones, I arrived home on the same date I left the ship.

In twenty-four hours, I went from standing watch in a 140-degree boiler room to below-zero temperatures in Minnesota. But I was finally stateside with Sandra and baby

Heide. We had about five months to enjoy one another's company before I would be redeployed.

Reuniting with Sandra after almost eight months and seeing little Heide for the first time—I know it had to be the most joyful moment. You'd think it would be unforgettable. However, this is a mental compartment that for some reason I can't open. Sandra also draws a complete blank of this time period and event. We remember nothing of our reunion at the airport, who drove us home, or seeing my parents and family, with whom we stayed while in Minnesota—nothing!

However, we do remember what happened next. Just a day or two after arrival, I became very ill. I had to be hospitalized and isolated for several days. Unable to digest food, I couldn't eat. I lost even more weight with only bags of saline as my diet.

After numerous tests, the doctor couldn't determine the problem. I was too sick to be scared, but Sandra was very frightened and was allowed to stay with me day and night. No one else was allowed in isolation.

After about a week I slowly recovered and was diagnosed with intestinal problems. These same problems would eventually lead to the removal of my large intestine and rectum in 1981 at the Mayo Clinic.

After being discharged from the hospital, I needed to purchase a car in Minnesota to drive to California, where the three of us would live. I asked Olaf to help me search for a car in good condition and in the price range Sandra and I could afford. I ended up buying a 1965 Chevelle.

Having a car would make our lives living off base in Alameda a lot easier. The ship would be docked at Hunters Point for two months for minor overhaul. The year before, I had to walk forty-five minutes in the dark every morning to catch the liberty launch from Alameda to the shipyard. This time around, I could drive. Life was looking up.

We packed the Chevelle with all the belongings we'd need for the next five months, then headed for California. We needed to be in Alameda soon, as the ship was due to pull in sometime during the next few days. I was required to report aboard upon its arrival.

Usually, when one aircraft carrier pulled into the States, another carrier pulled out. Thus, it was usually easy to find an apartment. However, when the *Hancock* returned to Hunters Point, so did the Big E. It needed repairs after the explosions on the flight deck. So the housing availability had tightened.

That night, in the rain, I was feeling heavy pressure on my shoulders as a husband, a new father, and a sailor trying to meet military demands. Sandra was strong, though. Her comfort and encouragement kept my weak moment in check and kept me focused on the task at hand.

Sandra, Heide, and I eventually reached Alameda in time, found an apartment, and settled in. Once the ship arrived, I was on four-section duty, meaning I was home three nights out of four and three weekends out of four.

At a young age, Sandra was an excellent cook, and I benefited from her good home cooking. I was gaining weight and getting decent rest. Our time together and with Heide was filled with love and enjoyment.

However, having to plan for my next deployment in less than five months was very much on our minds. The ship was scheduled to deploy for Vietnam at the end of July. We knew the next two months would pass quickly, with the ship scheduled for underway training and three-section duty in May. During our final three months together stateside, the ship would be in and out of port. That meant less time together, and Sandra would be alone with Heide in Alameda.

I received word that I had passed my machinist's mate

professional test. I looked forward to April, when I would sew on the E-4 machinist's mate emblem, which featured a crow and one chevron. The hard work on my first deployment had paid off. It meant an increase in military pay for me as well as an increased spousal allotment for Sandra—money that was much needed. It also meant no more working parties off-loading commissary supplies and bombs from supply ships.

March 28, 1969: President Eisenhower Dies

Honestly, I don't remember Eisenhower's death. I was busy with numerous challenges in front of me. I didn't have time to watch TV or sit down and read a newspaper. Free time was committed to Sandra and Heide. But from research many years later, I have learned about Eisenhower's role in leading us to the Vietnam War.

During World War II, Japan had taken control of Indochina, while France was failing in its attempt to reestablish colonial control of the region. The conflict was known as the First Indochina War.

In early 1954, Ho Chi Minh—a Vietnamese nationalist and a Communist—was on the verge of winning a stunning victory against French forces at the Battle of Dien Bien Phu. Eisenhower refused to commit American troops to the war. In a press conference, he stated, "I cannot conceive of a greater tragedy for America than to get heavily involved now in an all-out war in any of those regions." Eisenhower was right about one thing: it *was* a great tragedy.

In April 1954, the Geneva Accords resulted in the breakup of what had been French Indochina. It divided Vietnam at the seventeenth parallel. North of the parallel, Minh established a Democratic Republic of Vietnam under the rule of his Communist Lao Dong Party. In May, Dien Bien Phu officially fell.

South of the parallel, Ngo Dinh Diem, a strong anti-Communist Vietnamese nationalist, became the first president of the Republic of Vietnam.

Despite his initial statement about not intervening, Eisenhower was instrumental in escalating US involvement with Indo-Chinese internal affairs. Why? Word was, to stop the spread of Communism. Eisenhower likened it to a "falling domino" principle, which later became known as the domino theory. If one country fell to Communism, more would surely follow.

But there were undisclosed reasons as well. The Pentagon Papers revealed Eisenhower believed Indochina was vital to US security, power, and trade.

Though he sent no troops to the region, Eisenhower authorized military aid to the French—Americans' hard-earned tax dollars. The Eisenhower administration also aided Diem in consolidating power in Saigon. The United States began to engage in acts of sabotage and warfare in defense of South Vietnam. Throughout his second term as president, Eisenhower continued to support Diem's tyrannical regime. The two leaders met in 1957.

Later, in 1963, President Kennedy encouraged and directly assisted in Diem's overthrow. He was brutally killed. One day, an ally; the next, the enemy. My point is, American youth ended up in the Vietnam War because our political leaders led the United States down a rat hole.

April 15, 1969

Nixon had been president for less than three months when North Korea committed an act of war for the second time in less than two years. They shot down an American EC-121 four-engine turboprop reconnaissance plane operating over international waters one hundred miles off the coast of

North Korea. All thirty-one sailors aboard were killed.

In January, North Korea returned our severely beaten and tortured sailors from the USS *Pueblo*, and two months later, their fighter jets shot down a reconnaissance plane over international water. This was a direct challenge to President Nixon. And his response to counter such an egregious act of war? Nothing!

Below is a picture identical to the EC-121 North Korea shot down. Perhaps it'll trigger thoughts of how terrified those thirty-one sailors must have been when they were hit by an air-to-air missile fired by a North Korean pilot flying a Russian MiG. Imagine the last anxious thoughts of these brave young men as their plane spiraled out of control toward the ocean.

EC-121 turboprop

The tragedy of this event goes beyond the loss of life. How our government responded was a travesty as well.

When North Korea captured the USS *Pueblo* in January 1968, Nixon was still a private citizen eyeing the Republican ticket for the presidential race. Hearing of the capture, he was furious. He described it as a "tactical blunder" on the part of President Johnson. Which it was. This infuriated Johnson.

But after the attack on the EC-121, Nixon took Kissinger's advice and never retaliated for this act of war against the United States! Nixon choked. He had committed treason in 1968 because he wanted the presidency so bad. But when tested as president, he and Kissinger just kicked the can down the road. (And now, fifty years and nine presidents later, the United States might be on the brink of nuclear war with North Korea. What a bunch of bullshit!)

Neither Johnson nor Nixon retaliated against North Korea. Neither of them had the "backs" of those serving in the military. Each of us was just a number—my words! This is the reason the United States lost the Vietnam War. North Vietnam understood they were dealing with weak US leadership.

June 3, 1969

The destroyer USS *Frank E. Evans* was operating in the South China Sea between Saigon and the Spratly Islands with the Australian carrier HMAS *Melbourne*. The *Evans* had been providing plane guard for the US carriers on Yankee Station, and then it was redirected to take up plane guard and rescue position for the *Melbourne* as it prepared for night-flying operations.

At around 0300 on June 3, the *Melbourne* signaled the *Evans* to prepare to take up position one thousand yards behind the *Melbourne*. It was the fifth time that night the *Evans* was to carry out this maneuver.

The sea was dead calm, and the water moonlit. The *Melbourne* had her navigation lights at full brilliance. Procedures had been clearly established for the *Evans*, the smaller vessel, to turn to port, away from the *Melbourne*, before falling into a position well behind.

But the *Evans* mistakenly turned to starboard—into the path of the *Melbourne*'s bow. Approximately ninety feet of the bow of the *Evans* was severed completely. The bow section sank, and seventy-four US sailors were killed.

I'm sure these very tired sailors had been sleeping in the forward compartments, only to be awaken to a miserable death. As mentioned in chapter 8, their story is told in the book *American Boys*.

War is hell. In the navy, you didn't fear injury or death from hand-to-hand combat with or gunfire from the enemy. When you were in combat operations at sea, you were very cognizant of injury or death due to shipboard casualties. You feared fires, suffocation, drowning, ruptured steam lines, kinetic energy from flying metal, and more. Awareness of the danger of human error kept me from getting complacent. It gave me a strong focus on the task at hand.

Remains of the USS Evans *forward compartments*
For me, every time I descended the ladder into the engine

room or boiler room, I knew there was the danger of a boiler explosion, a main steam line rupture, or an oil fire. I knew I could be literally cooked like a piece of meat or boiled like a lobster. I didn't dwell on it because I had a duty to do, but it was always in the back of my mind.

And once again, here's the real kick in the ass: the seventy-four sailors who lost their lives that night were *not* considered victims of the Vietnam War by the US Department of Defense. Therefore, their names do not appear on the Wall.

This was the *Evans*'s fourth deployment to Vietnam. She had just completed "Operation Daring Rebel" in May, providing naval gun support off the coast of Da Nang. However, the *Melbourne* was not in the "combat zone" and was only providing reconnaissance support to the United States, rather than flying combat strikes against Vietnam. For this reason, the *Evans* was technically not in the "combat zone" even though they were operating in the South China Sea off the coast of Saigon.

It's my belief that these deaths—and all the deaths in that trumped-up war—were caused by the leaders of the United States government, to whom the American people had entrusted their vote.

June 1969

LeRoy, the first class in charge of the aft engine room, achieved the rank of chief petty officer. I received my start under Chief LeRoy. He was a friend. Stateside, we'd gather with our wives for friendship, and our wives would support each other when the ship was at sea.

Chief LeRoy was heavily schooled and well seasoned in the engine room. He was responsible for maintaining operational readiness and keeping all those serving under his command safe from casualties.

As I look back, I realize Chief LeRoy and Mr. Schmuck, the M Division officer, both played a huge roll in the operational readiness of the crew and the engine room. As much as I rail on Mr. Schmuck, I must admit he was very knowledgeable of engine and boiler operation. Both he and Chief LeRoy applied safety standards in the engine room, ensuring no major injuries or casualties.

June 27, 1969

Life magazine printed portraits of all 249 Americans killed in Vietnam during the previous two weeks, including the forty-six killed at Hamburger Hill. These once-smiling young faces of the dead had a stunning impact on Americans nationwide.

Remember Johnson's words about "how the mothers weep"? Imagine what the mothers, fathers, and other family members did as they opened that magazine to view their loved ones.

Hamburger Hill was especially grisly and vicious. The fortified Hill 937 in the A Shau Valley near Hue was of little strategic value. However, US command ordered a frontal assault on the hill—and a fierce ten-day battle ensued. The machine gun fire was so intense, someone said it was like being inside a hamburger machine or a meat grinder.

Days after its capture, US command abandoned it. Unforgivable.

July 11, 1969

After a short yard period at Hunters Point for repairs, the USS *Hancock* was back at sea, conducting training exercises in preparation for another deployment in late July. Even though we were not in combat operation yet, danger was still around every corner.

An F-8 jet experienced a hydraulic failure and came in too low during night landing exercises. The LTJG pilot ejected just before the aircraft crashed into the rounddown. The jet split into two pieces, which hurtled down the flight deck and erupted into a massive fuel-fed fire.

No sailors were killed, but damage to the flight deck was extensive. It resulted in a frantic 24-7 repair effort to keep the ship on schedule for deployment.

The *Hancock* avoided another disaster.

July 20, 1969

At 1:18 p.m., the *Apollo 11* lunar modules landed on the moon. This was a big event not only for the United States but for the whole world.

Several days in my life are ingrained in my memory: my wedding, the killing of President Kennedy, the *Challenger* explosion after liftoff, collapse of the World Trade Center towers. The lunar landing, however, is ingrained because I did something crazy while it was happening.

First, I left the apartment and walked across the street to a grocery store. Understand, this was a four-lane street, a main artery with heavy traffic throughout the day. But there wasn't a car in sight as far as I could see in either direction. I couldn't believe my eyes. When I came out of the grocery store, in which I was the only customer, I still saw no cars in either direction.

So to commemorate the moon landing, and while everyone—I mean *everyone*—was sitting in front of their televisions, I lay flat on my back right in the middle of that four-lane road. Dumb, but a lasting memory in those final days before my second deployment.

Chapter 10
Second Deployment to Vietnam

Oiler suppling fuel to the Hancock *and her escort in transit to Vietnam.*

Saying goodbye and knowing it'd be eight months before I would see Sandra and Heide again—it felt like it'd be eternity. What made it hard was knowing that this would not be my last deployment. It was only my second. That meant we would have to go through this gut-wrenching separation again.

I'd been in the navy for two years, and I had another two years until discharge. Again, it was an eternity. I never thought about going AWOL, but I understood why some sailors made that decision.

July 30, 1969

Dear Sandra,

I watched you and Heide board the plane for Minnesota. It was the hardest thing I've done. I sat in the car and cried.

Floyd and Marie said I could park my car at their house, and Marie would give me a ride to the base. So I dropped my car off at Marie and Floyd's and stayed for supper. We ate in the dining room again, and I didn't even knock any food off my plate.

A year earlier, my cousin Marie and her husband, Floyd, had asked Sandra and I to join them and their friends for dinner on a Sunday afternoon. Their friends were established doctors, as was Floyd. Marie had the table set with fine china, silverware, and a white tablecloth. Very elegant and formal.

As I looked at the table setting, this was an oh-shit moment. As in, *oh shit—I haven't been schooled on etiquette and the formality before my eyes.* I would have to wing it.

As Sandra and I sat at the table, we listened to Floyd and his friend complimenting each other on their most recently performed surgeries. I remained quiet. My most recent work experience was firefighting school at the Treasure Island

Naval Base. I didn't think it rose to the level of the verbal praise being passed around the table. However, as I look back now, I think they might have appreciated my thoughts on firefighting skills used to save the ship and the lives aboard.

I tried to mimic the other guests' etiquette so I wouldn't stand out like a black hair on a white pig. When I picked up my knife and fork to clumsily cut my baked potato, I knocked the damn thing on the floor. Not saying a word, I reached down, picked it up, put it on my plate, and continued to cut it up.

No one said a word. Life goes on.

August 2, 1969
Dear Sandra,

The ship left Alameda for Vietnam via Hawaii. We've hit bad weather. The ship is really rocking and rolling.

August 4, 1969
Dear Sandra,

I changed my military allotment, and you'll receive $250 per month.

Good news too—I have less than two years left in the navy.

Over the 1MC, the captain said we'll have a stop in the PIs for two days, and then we'll sail straight to the Gulf of Tonkin for line duty.

I'm scheduled to take the machinist mate second class test on August 7, with results posted the first week of October.

August 6, 1969
Dear Sandra,

I'm standing break-in watch for assistant top watch. Standing mostly four-and-eight watches. Sometimes four-

and-four, but no more working parties now that I'm a third class.

August 8, 1969

Dear Sandra,

Heading to Hawaii. It's been a steady diet of general quarter drills. The captain wants the ship's crew ready for combat operations upon arriving off the coast of Vietnam.

August 11, 1969

Dear Sandra,

The ship almost pulled out of Hawaii with only a skeleton crew. An earthquake near the Kuril Islands prompted a tsunami warning for Hawaii. The captain had been advised of a possible tidal wave. A tidal wave would swamp the ship.

While in Hawaii, I stood by for my friend Bubble Butt. He had a commissary working party, so I had to take his assigned duty. However, as a third-class petty officer, I didn't have to work or lift boxes. I just sat and made sure everybody else worked. A far cry from my last deployment.

Bubble Butt was only five six but all muscle. He was the ship's weightlifting champion on the 1967 deployment to Vietnam. Strong as an ox, he was the California state wrestling champion in his weight division. We called him Bubble Butt because his butt, which was all muscle, stood out. I never saw him in action, but the word was, when he'd get into a fight at a bar, he would jump up on a chair or table to equalize the height difference, and one punch later, the other guy was done.

August 13, 1969

Dear Sandra,

The ship left Hawaii and is steaming for the PIs. The captain has informed the crew that general quarters will sound tomorrow at 0400—not fun.

August 14, 1969

Dear Sandra,

General quarters were maintained for twelve hours today. C rations were passed out to feed the engine room. I was standing booster and condensate pump watch on the lower level, and I exchanged the cigarettes in my C ration for candy.

No one could leave the engine room during general quarters. It's my memory that the C rations were delivered to the engine room via the escape hatch located on the lower level, behind the Number 8 fire pump. The main hatch remained closed, though.

One more memory: the crackers in the C ration packs would swell up to four times their size when in water. So, a couple of crackers took care of your hunger.

August 19, 1969

Dear Sandra,

The ship crossed the date line today. I'm another day older and never saw August 18. We went from Sunday the seventeenth to Tuesday the nineteenth.

Mr. Schmuck is M Division's senior officer. This billet is usually staffed with a lieutenant-grade line officer. Scuttlebutt is, Mr. Schmuck was up for warrant officer three. However, he's still wearing a warrant officer two symbol. He's as ornery as ever and still smoking the same dirty pipe.

August 22, 1969

Dear Sandra,

The captain announced tropical working hours. On this deployment, Mr. Schmuck is going easy on the crew and not making us work during tropical hours. I can't believe it! Those extra three or four hours of downtime makes life a little less miserable.

August 23, 1969

Dear Sandra,

I have seven hundred days left in the navy.

I heard a good one today: in the chow line, a sailor took his wife's used Kotex out of a plastic bag, put it onto his tray, had gravy poured over it, walked to the mess area, sat down, and proceeded to eat it. He was written up on a general article of the UCMJ (United States Code of Military Justice). He must of had a bet with a buddy. What next!

August 25, 1969

Dear Sandra,

There are smoker boxing matches in the hanger bay. This is something new.

"Smokers" were special boxing matches put on as entertainment while at sea.

August 26, 1969

Dear Sandra,

Got my shot card updated today. I received another air gun shot in the arm. Again, it didn't hurt until I walked away, and then it about knocked me on my ass. I think it hit the bone—too much air pressure.

August 27, 1969

Dear Sandra,

Pulled into the PIs today and will pull out on the twenty-ninth for a thirty-day line period.

August 29, 1969

Dear Sandra,

I'm so tired—haven't had much sleep in the last seventy-two hours due to breakdowns. Just heard there's a problem on the Number 4 generator, and I expect I'll be called to help repair.

August 30, 1969

Dear Sandra,

My second class and I overhauled the condensate pump on the Number 4 generator. I've been crawling around in the Number 4 fireroom's bilges all night. It took me a half hour to clean up. My hands are swollen, and one finger has a big blood blister where I pinched it between the outer casing and the main housing of the pump. I bet I sweated off three gallons of water—it was hot.

The ship service turbo generator condensate pump

A picture is worth a thousand words in telling my story. It's an extreme struggle to repair the condensate pump when underway at sea. The pump is located on the lower level of the Number 4 fireroom. With both boilers operating at capacity, the boiler room is over 120 degrees. The area is poorly lit, and the pump hosing is under the deck plates, called the bilges.

After removing the deck plates to access the pump housing, you had to crawl down in the bilges between the metal frame system holding the deck plates. There was no air movement, it was dark, and you were working with only a droplight. It was slippery, greasy, and dirty from decades of standing black oil. Everything was hot to the touch.

Your assignment was to dismantle the condensate pump,

exposing the internal components that have excessive wear or are completely broken. You then made repairs and reassembled the pump. After the first hour, your clothes were soaking wet from sweat and your hands were filthy and swollen from wrenching and removing the outer pump casting. You were tired, but time was critical, and the pressure was on.

I remember repairing the condensate pump with my second class. I was tired from little sleep the prior day. I watched him place a wad of chew under his lip. He knew I was short on sleep, so he asked if I wanted a chew. He said it would keep me awake.

I didn't smoke and had never tried chewing tobacco, but I thought, *What the hell?* I reached into his container of chew, grabbed a pinch, and put it between my lower lip and teeth, as I'd seen my uncle Ray do many times.

About sixty seconds later, my head was spinning, and I thought I would pass out. Another oh-shit moment. I couldn't spit the entire wad out fast enough. I can still see that half smile on my second class's face as my head was spinning. He didn't say much, didn't ask if I was okay—just continued to repair the pump. It was the last time I ever tried chewing tobacco.

September 1, 1969

Dear Sandra,

I'm sitting on station Number 6 as I write this letter. It's windy but feels good. Really good. It's the first time I've been topside and alone since pulling out of the PIs. I can finally think about you, Heide, and home.

The Pacific commander, Chief Admiral McCain, is coming aboard, so the ship has to be squared away. Something is going on. The commander of the Pacific fleet doesn't just decide to visit the USS Hancock *without a very high level of need.*

Remember: 694 days left in the navy.

As I look back, I believe Admiral McCain came aboard to ready the *Hancock* for Nixon's upcoming Madman Strategy event. This highly sensitive information would have been delivered only in person to the *Hancock*'s captain—not by electronic communication, for fear of enemy intercept. There's more about the Madman Strategy to come.

September 2, 1969

Ho Chi Minh died of a heart attack at the age of seventy-nine. He was succeeded by Le Duan, first secretary to the Vietnam Worker's Party. At the funeral, Le Duan publicly read Ho's will and testament, as Ho had anticipated his own death. His will stated, "We must maintain our resolve to fight the Yankee attackers until we achieve total victory."

10, 1969

Dear Sandra,

Mr. Schmuck held another seabag inspection. This time, I passed. Every time he's senior division officer, he has a seabag inspection. He's an asshole who just screws with the troops.

September 15, 1969

Dear Sandra,

Not much happening on the ship lately, just the same old bullshit. Eat, sleep, work, and stand watch.

September 16, 1969

Dear Sandra,

The ship is replenishing after flight operations today, taking on food, fuel, and ammo. It sure is nice not having to muster for a working party.

September 17, 1969

Dear Sandra,

A plane crashed on the flight deck last night and wrecked another two planes. I haven't heard if anyone was killed.

As it turned out, no one was killed in this crash. Lucky.

September 18, 1969

Dear Sandra,

Two guys from another ship are sleeping in our compartment. This is strange. Word is that they're under-cover, looking for drugs and drug users.

September 25, 1969

Dear Sandra,

Pulling into the PIs tomorrow. The word is, we're picking up a few more jets before we head to Vietnam.

September 30, 1969

On this date, Daniel Ellsberg made the decision to make several copies of the seven-thousand-page Pentagon Papers, which he would later release to the *New York Times*. This is also discussed in chapter 1, but I will add two thoughts here:

1. Ellsberg was wrong to turn over a top-secret document to the *New York Times*. He knew it was wrong. He mentally struggled with the thought of his children visiting him in jail if convicted. But he also knew American youth were dying in an immoral war, so he exposed the documents even at the risk of conviction.

2. The Pentagon Papers indicate that several presidents misled and even lied to the American people and Congress—which I consider equally wrong. With the release of the papers, these leaders were exposed for unjust acts that caused 58,000 military deaths.

October 1, 1969

Dear Sandra,

The ship pulled out of the PIs, heading for Vietnam and a thirty-day line period.

My second class and three other friends got into a fight with a group of marines. The second class busted the nose and smashed the face of some unlucky marine.

October 5, 1969

Dear Sandra,

I was up until 0200 participating in operational drills. I'm very tired. The USS Constellation *is on the line with the* Hancock, *and I heard they lost a C-2 COD.*

October 12, 1969

Dear Sandra,

Bad news: scuttlebutt says the Hancock *has been extended an extra month on this deployment. If correct, this will make for a long deployment.*

October 17, 1969

Dear Sandra,

One of our F-8s shot down a MiG. Also, an F-8 from the Hancock *was in a dogfight with two MiGs, and one of the MiGs shot an air-to-air missile at our F-8. The pilot of the F-8 went into a roll straight down to avoid the missile. He pulled up just before hitting the ground, which made the missile run into the ground—lucky.*

There was a smoker on the hanger bay today—the Oriskany *against the* Hancock. *These events are for those who are short on work, but the engine rooms are working overtime.*

October 18, 1969
Dear Sandra,

I burned my left shoulder bad on a steam line while lighting off the Number 3 generator. Big bubble of fluid under the skin. If I hadn't had a long-sleeve shirt on, I would have left the skin on the steam line. Sick bay packed it with ice, then put a dressing on it with a solution. I report back to sick bay tomorrow to change the dressing.

October 19, 1969
Dear Sandra,

Just received an airmail letter from you dated October 1—mail is a little slow.

October 20, 1969
Dear Sandra,

I went up to sick bay today to have the dressing changed again. They pulled the dead skin off and wiped it with a solution. SOB!

October 21, 1969
Dear Sandra,

Your last letter said Heide is walking from room to room. That would be fun to see.

I went to sick bay to have my dressing changed again. My burn isn't healing. Sick bay told me the engine room is too humid. No shit! However, they didn't offer me a no-duty or even a light-duty chit to present to Mr. Schmuck.

October 23, 1969
Dear Sandra,

I have very good news! I passed my test and made second class petty officer. I sew on the second chevon on December 16. Unbelievable! Only one other M Division machinist's mate passed the E-5 test this rating period. You'll receive an allotment increase of $45 per month.

Three years ago, we were in high school, going steady, and falling in love. I would have never imagined this path in our lives. It has been difficult and demanding, and we still have another deployment before I'm discharged. But this was meant to be, and we're standing tall.

October 26, 1969
Dear Sandra,

Mr. Schmuck received orders and will be leaving soon—no loss.

October 27, 1969
Dear Sandra,

The ship is steaming toward Japan for R & R. The temperature is dropping, so the engine room is cooling down. It should be about fifty or sixty degrees in Sasebo. The captain expects to pull into Sasebo on the thirty-first.

Three years ago today, we started going steady.

October 1969
In October 1969, President Nixon was hell-bent on bringing North Vietnam to the negotiating table to end the war. And so the Madman Strategy may have brought us closer

to nuclear war than the Cuban Missile Crisis in 1962.

Nixon and Kissinger believed they could compel North Vietnam to back down via intimidation. They had a plan to make North Vietnam—and the Soviet Union—believe Nixon was "crazy" enough to use nuclear weapons. Nixon told H. R. Haldeman, his chief of staff, to send a message to the North Vietnamese: "We'll just slip the word to them that 'For God's sake, you know Nixon is obsessed about Communism. We can't restrain him when he's angry—and he has his hand on the nuclear button."

On October 10, Nixon and Kissinger put the plan in motion, sending the Strategic Air Command (SAC) an urgent order to prepare for a possible confrontation. They wanted the most powerful thermonuclear weapons in the United States arsenal readied for immediate use against the Soviet Union. Known as the Joint Chiefs of Staff (JCS) Readiness Test, the plan involved strategic bombers, tactical air, and a variety of naval operations, including the movement of Task Force Seventy-Seven in the Gulf of Tonkin.

Nixon wanted his adversaries to think he was irrational and volatile. In fact, many of Nixon's allies and own military leaders were left thinking the same thing. The mission was so secretive that even the senior military officers following the orders—including the SAC commander himself—were not informed of its true purpose!

Let that sink in: the US military senior officers were operating under the assumption that they were actually preparing for a nuclear war. With 30 percent of the military on drugs and many more suffering from a don't-give-a-shit attitude, the Madman Strategy was a recipe for a disaster. One accident, one miscommunication within the United States military, and/or one preemptive defensive strike from the Soviet Union would have started an all-out nuclear war. Nixon was nuts, and so was that intellectual idiot, Kissinger!

As I think back, I believe the *Hancock* was part of Nixon's JCS Readiness Test. I remember watching armed marines line up and stand guard as different-looking bombs were brought through the mess hall to the elevator supporting the hanger deck. These white bombs were much smaller than the usual 250-pound green bombs I helped move during working parties on my first cruise. I had never seen these bombs, nor had I seen armed marines guarding ammunition. I later learned that the smaller white bombs were indeed tactical nuclear weapons.

Needless to say, Nixon's Madman Strategy didn't work. North Vietnam had no intention of negotiating or ending the war without victory; they were willing to fight to the death. Russia did not intend to stop supplying North Vietnam with military equipment and arms. And the United States was *not* willing to "decapitate the head of the snake" and defeat North Vietnam to secure victory.

In the end, the United States simply gave up and went home, leaving South Vietnam to suffer an agonizing loss. Sounds harsh, but that's the nonpolitical way to state it.

November 3, 1969
Dear Sandra,
   My shoulder is completely healed—but tender.

November 13, 1969
Dear Sandra,
   When I get out, I'm going to tell this outfit to kiss my rosy red ass.

(I must have been having a bad day!)

November 17, 1969

Dear Sandra,

The word is, the ship will pull into Alameda on April 12, 1970. The bad news is, the ship leaves again for Vietnam on September 12, 1970. Only five months in the States, and three of those will be for underway training and three-section duty.

November 28, 1969

Dear Sandra,

Lost another plane today. An F-8 hit the rounddown when landing and crashed. The LT ejected, escaped the wreckage, and was recovered.

November 29, 1969

Dear Sandra,

The ship is heading north toward Sasebo. Interesting— the ship is spending less time on the line this cruise. The XO has provided the remainder of the ship's deployment:

December 31 to January 3: in port, Sasebo
January 4 to January 10: special operation
January 11 to January 16: in port, Hong Kong
January 17 to January 31: line period
February 1 to February 12: line period
February 15 to February 21: in port, Sasebo
February 22 to February 25: special operations
February 26 February 28: in port, Sasebo
March 1 to March 27: line period
March 28 to March 29: in port, PIs
March 30: steaming to Alameda
April 5: cross date line
April 12: arrive in Alameda

December 1, 1969

The first draft lottery since World War II was held in New York City. Capsules representing each day of the year were selected at random and assigned a draft order number from 001 to 365. Those with low numbers would likely be drafted.

Prior to the lottery, the US government gave exemptions to young men who were in college, married, had political connections, had sore toes, etc. The exemption allowed families with political influence, money, and/or higher test scores to keep their sons from the draft. President Clinton and President Trump are both good examples.

The way it was implemented, the draft was totally unfair. Many of those drafted into ground troops were young men that were from low-income families and/or had low test scores. And of those drafted, many were unable to pass military entrance exams allowing them to enlist in a branch of the service other than the army. A majority of these draftees were sent to the jungles of Vietnam.

As of December 1, 1969, the day of the lottery draft, over 40,000 men had been killed in the Vietnam War.

December 10, 1969

Dear Sandra,

I'm now qualifying for top watch in the engine rooms. I'll have a lot of additional responsibilities as a second -class machinist's mate when I'm rated on the sixteenth.

Remember my first time at sea in April 1968, when an emergency developed and scared the shit out of me? From that point forward, it was my goal to gain the knowledge and rank to be in control of the engine room and my own destiny. Know it's not only to ensure my safety but also to ensure the safety of all those reporting to me in the engine room.

December 11, 1969
Dear Sandra,

Just got out of the aft engine room. Long hours. Had trouble with the Number 3 main engine.

December 12, 1969
Dear Sandra,

A second-class machinist's mate lifer came aboard and was assigned to the aft engine room. He's bunking below me in the berthing compartment. He's been in the navy nine years and just shipped over for another four years. He's as dumb as a box of rocks when it comes to the operation of the engine room. How the hell did he make second class? He's under my direction, and I'm technically still a third class. He's never qualified for top watch, and I don't think he'll qualify for assistant top watch. Worthless and dangerous. If the navy gave him $10,000 to ship over, they got screwed.

During the Vietnam War, the navy offered second-class machinist's mates $10,000 bonuses to ship over. Also, you were assured all the powdered eggs, potatoes, milk, and more you could eat or drink while at sea.

December 16, 1969
Dear Sandra,

I'm now a second-class petty officer. When in Sasebo, I had my second-class crow and two chevons sewn onto all my uniforms. I purchased new shirts and had them laundered with medium starch. I had them and my pants pressed.

Standing four hours on and eight hours off. Life is better.

At my semiannual performance review, my superiors gave me the highest marks for my appearance and the wearing of my uniform. I took great pride in my uniform, and I wore it with respect. How you looked and how you carried yourself had a major impact on how you were perceived by those who reported to you and by those to whom you reported.

I had sixteen sets of dungarees that I had cleaned, starched, and pressed each time we were in port, which provided me a clean uniform every other day. In comparison, most enlisted sailors had their uniforms cleaned via the ship's laundry. Their dungarees returned to the compartment looking as faded and wrinkled as a worn-out rag. Again, when you put on one of these uniforms, you too looked like a worn-out rag, or a sloppy bum off the street.

I still remember reporting for the midnight watch and sliding down the hand rails of the ladder to the aft engine room, the second chevon on my left sleeve. A friend was the first to notice the crow and the second chevon. He provided a traditional navy initiation custom: a right fist to the shoulder as hard as one could. It was all in good fun, but by the end of the day, my shoulder was black-and-blue. I was proud.

December 17, 1969

Dear Sandra,

Lost another plane last night. The LT was flying a mission over Vietnam when his F-8 was hit by enemy fire. He headed out to sea for an easier rescue but crashed seventy-five miles off the coast, in the Gulf of Tonkin. His body was not recovered.

All crew members had to report to sick bay for shots today. Had to get the shots before we pulled into Hong Kong. So, I've got two sore arms. One of the shots was in my already sore arm, where everybody hit me as initiation for advancement to second class.

December 18, 1969

Dear Sandra,

The ship left Yankee Station heading for the PIs to drop off a couple of planes. We pulled in for two hours and then headed for Sasebo. I'll call you on the twenty-third.

December 19, 1969

Dear Sandra,

The ship is now heading to Sasebo, Japan. The captain came over the 1MC and said life jackets are required out on the weather decks. Twelve-to-fifteen-foot sea with fifty-mile-an-hour wind. The ship is rocking and rolling.

Mr. Schmuck called me down to M Division office and drilled me on the operation of the engine room's top watch duties. Nailed the questions.

He was supposed to get off the ship before this deployment but didn't. Then he was supposed to get off this month but was extended to April. I don't feel sorry for the lifer, but I feel sorry for his wife.

I remember sitting in the M Division office for several hours as Mr. Schmuck quizzed me on all the duties and responsibilities of the engine room's top watch billet—making sure I could handle stress under pressure. He left no stone unturned.

As I think back, I understand his responsibility was to ensure I was thoroughly qualified to manage the duties of top watch before he signed off on my paperwork. The future of his advancement was on the line.

He fully understood I was young—twenty years old—and had been in the navy for only two and a half years. And he was about to sign his name on a document giving me responsibility and authority in a critical position in one of two engine rooms of an aircraft carrier pushed to its limit during combat operations off the coast of Vietnam.

December 20, 1969

Dear Sandra,

We're a day late pulling into Sasebo due to high winds and heavy seas. The ship has been steaming at only 10 knots because the destroyers ("tin cans") can't keep up. I'd hate to be riding in a tin can during this storm. We're up to 20 knots now, and the ship is rocking and rolling all over the place. I was told the waves are breaking over the flight deck.

Mr. Schmuck was making small talk with me, which was a first. He cracks me up. He really thinks the navy needs him and that shitty pipe he smokes. I just shook my head yes and smiled.

I was going to stand by for a shipmate in Hong Kong, but Mr. Schmuck shot down my shipmate's request. Mt. Schmuck has heard of my shipmate's past nights on the town in previous ports—booze and prostitutes!

My brother Paul was stationed in Hawaii as a second-class communications petty officer. He was monitoring communication between Task Force Seventy-Seven and the Seventh Fleet command in Hawaii during this storm. Later, in the 1970s, he told me that during this storm, the destroyer escort following the *Hancock* had listed, or rolled, beyond the degree it was designed to withstand. It should have tipped over. Paul also told me he was aware of the *Hancock*'s movement when I was deployed to Vietnam.

January 1, 1970—New Year's Day

Dear Sandra,

The ship is in port at Sasabo. Pulling out tomorrow and

heading for Hong Kong. My plans are to have two dress suits and a set of dress blue gabardines handmade in Hong Kong.

January 4, 1970
Dear Sandra,

I went ashore and was measured for several suits and a set of gabardines.

January 7, 1970
Dear Sandra,

It's for sure—the ship has been extended two additional days. We'll pull into the States on April 14.

January 16, 1970
Dear Sandra,

Picked up my tailor-made suits today in Hong Kong. Before leaving the ship, we had to exchange US dollars for "funny money." We can't take US dollars off the ship. The exchange rate is $1.75 US for 10 Hong Kong dollars. A show in Hong Kong cost three and a half Hong Kong dollars.

January 17, 1970
Dear Sandra,

The Hancock *pulled out of Hong Kong today and headed for line duty.*

January 18, 1970
Dear Sandra,

Good news: because of my outstanding performance this deployment, I've been selected again to fly off the ship on early leave! Don't know any details yet.

January 23, 1970

Dear Sandra,

Back on tropical working hours again. But these hours no longer have much effect on me, now that I'm a second class. No working parties, no cleaning the bilges, no shining the brass, etc. Life is much easier. However, I'm the go-to for repairs on the generators and the aft engine room equipment.

January 27, 1970

Dear Sandra,

The ship is on reduced water usage—we lost an evaporator. Orders have been given for seamen's shower only.

Bubble Butt got written up by the master-at-arms for taking a ten-minute shower. Doesn't sound like they'll send him to captain's mast, though. He's to be rated as a third-class petty officer in February, which M Division needs. They also need him on throttles.

February 1, 1970

Dear Sandra,

Captain came over the closed-circuit TV and said the ship pulls into Alameda April 16, then moves over to Hunters Point shipyard for two months, then starts underway training and deploys back to Vietnam in August.

February 3, 1970

Dear Sandra,

It's our second anniversary! I'm sitting out on station Number 6 writing this letter. It's getting dark. There's a beautiful sunset, and it's very peaceful with just the sound of the waves lapping at the side of the ship as it moves through

*the ocean. I'm thinking about our wedding and about seeing
you and Heide again in April.*

February 4, 1970
Dear Sandra,

*One of the men on the ship came down with TB
(tuberculosis), so they flew him off the ship. Now everybody
on the ship is required to have a TB shot. Just received mine.*

February 5, 1970
Dear Sandra,

*As second class, I've been assigned as petty officer in
charge of the Number 3 and 4 ship service turbo generators.
I'm responsible for operation, repairs, and maintenance. M
Division chief told me I'll fly off the ship March 15 for early
leave.*

February 7, 1970
Dear Sandra,

*M Division posted the duty schedule for when the ship
pulls into the States. The ship will shift to four-section duty,
and I've been assigned as M Division section leader.*

*I'm writing this letter topside. When I look out, what I see
is where the water meets the sky. It's a big world—I'm so far
from home.*

February 8, 1970
Dear Sandra,

*We lost a helicopter today. It was flying alongside the
ship and went down for some reason. There were seven men
aboard. One jumped out at about forty feet in the air and was
hurt. Another chipped his teeth. And the others came out
unhurt. The* Hancock *pulled alongside the helicopter and*

picked it out of the ocean with the B & A (boat and aircraft) crane.

The airdale I met at the 2016 Veterans Day ceremony served aboard the ship during this deployment. He remembered this event as well. He told me the helicopter was hovering alongside the ship when it broke in half and fell into the ocean. Airdales worked the hanger bay and flight deck, so they were much more informed about accidents in these areas of the ship.

February 9, 1970
Dear Sandra,
I performed preventive maintenance on the Number 4 generator all morning. We had a stand-down for the remainder of the day, and the captain gave the ship holiday routine. I have the afternoon off.
Lost another pilot and plane today.

The LT was completing a bombing run over South Vietnam when a bomb became jammed under his plane. He diverted to Da Nang, rather than the carrier, for landing. Upon landing, the plane blew a tire and the bomb exploded, killing the LT. If he had landed on the ship, it certainly would have been a disaster.

February 10, 1970
Dear Sandra,
I put in a chit for early leave today.

February 11, 1970
Dear Sandra,
The USS Ranger *and the USS* Oriskany *were extended to*

eleven months. That's a long deployment. Bad news for them; good news for the Hancock.

February 15, 1970

Dear Sandra,

To hear your voice was such an uplift. [I called Sandra long-distance from Sasebo. We talked for eight minutes, costing twenty-two dollars.] *It gave me the drive and push to mentally stay focused. I look forward to returning home and holding you again.*

The second class being discharged leaves the ship on February 18, and two third-class aft engine room machinist's mates leave on the nineteenth and the twenty-first. I spent a lot of time in the engine room with these three sailors. It's interesting that the second class leaves on my twenty-first birthday, and I was assigned his responsibilities in M Division. The third class's wife, Kathy, hasn't had their baby yet.

The ship was awarded the Battle "E" (Battle Efficiency Award). Of all the aircraft carriers serving combat operations in Vietnam, the USS Hancock *was honored for the best performance. This allows the crew of the* Hancock *to wear the "E" patch on their left shoulder.*

The captain and XO paint the Battle "E" on the side of the ship.

This was such a big accomplishment because the USS *Hancock* was a twenty-six-year-old World War II aircraft carrier. It was competing for the "E" against newer super-carriers such as the USS *America*, the USS *Ranger*, and the USS *Kitty Hawk*, as well as against a nuclear carrier, the USS *Enterprise*.

The USS *Hancock* was the smallest attack aircraft carrier in the Seventh Fleet. Attack carriers were equipped with angled decks and steam catapults, and they were identified with "CVA" before their numbers. In fact, the USS *Hancock* was the first aircraft carrier in the United States fleet equipped with an angled deck and steam catapults.

In a small way, I contributed to the USS *Hancock*'s Battle "E." I felt a sense of self-satisfaction and pride wearing the "E" patch on my shoulder. The "E" represented the hard work and dedication of those who served aboard the USS *Hancock*. Again, the operation of a warship is a "team sport." And if someone drops the ball, it means more than losing a game. It can mean losing lives in a disaster.

February 16, 1970

Sandra left Minnesota for California to await my early leave arrival. I started sending my letters to Floyd and Marie's address in Oakland.

February 18, 1970

Dear Sandra,

Today I turned twenty-one years old.

The ship is conducting wartime operations off the coast of Vietnam. I've risen to the rank of second-class machinist's mate, standing top watch in the aft engine room. I'm responsible for orders issued from the bridge and main control, and I'm in charge of the Number 2 engine room and crew during wartime deployment. I'm one of only a few enlisted machinist's mates to achieve the rank of E-5 in less than two years. Very proud.

February 22, 1970

Dear Sandra,

The ship pulls into Sasebo today. The second class was to leave the ship on the eighteenth but leaves today and will be discharged in the States. The M Division officer dropped all the second class's responsibilities on me. The second class was a hell of a mentor. I'm very grateful.

February 23, 1970
Dear Sandra,

All top watches are now standing four hours on, twelve hours off. For me, life is now bearable at sea. However, my awareness of the miserable life of a non-rate does not go unnoticed, as I manage their engine room duties with concern for their well-being.

February 24, 1970
Dear Sandra,

Messenger woke me at 2330 and reported trouble with the Number 3 generator. I had to go down to the boiler room and fix the problem. By the time I finished the repairs, it was time to go stand the 0400 to 0800 top watch in the aft engine room. No complaints—I'm getting proper sleep.

February 25, 1970
Dear Sandra,

Messenger woke me at 0230 to check on a spring bearing problem.

February 28, 1970
Dear Sandra,

Received your letter saying you found an apartment for $190 per month, including furniture. That was good news. It sure was nice of Marie to help you look for an apartment.

March 1, 1970
Dear Sandra,

The steam condensate pump in the aft engine room broke

down—had to repair it today.

Mr. Schmuck leaves for the States today. M Division has a new division officer. He's a young lieutenant, college educated, didn't come up through the ranks of the enlisted as Mr. Schmuck did. Hopefully he's not an asshole who smokes a shitty pipe.

March 3, 1970
Dear Sandra,

This is my last letter of this deployment. I'll be flying off the ship soon. Mr. Schmuck is gone—no tears.

Chapter 11

Stateside: 1970

Heide at two years and four months

March 1970

I remember preparing my seabag in the compartment and making my way up to the flight deck to be flown off the *Hancock* on March 10. I stepped out on the flight deck— only to find that the plane had already left. I was told I could catch a flight off the ship the next day.

Needless to say, I was disappointed. To this day, I still don't understand what happened. Through all my time in the navy, I had never been late. And that wasn't the best time to experience a first.

The next day, I was finally catapulted off the ship. We headed to Subic Bay in the PIs. There, I caught a naval transport bus for a fifty-mile ride to Clark Air Base. The bus trip wound through the countryside and small towns. I remember seeing farmers plowing their fields with oxen. The farmers' homes were huts with straw roofs and no windows.

In one small town, we approached a four-way stop on dirt streets, yet there was an officer directing traffic. I looked out the window to see Filipino men kneeling in a circle, watching a cockfight. A first.

When I arrived at Clark Air Base, I entered my name on a list to get a military hop to Travis Air Force Base in California. The bad news: there was a long waiting list. I was told it'd be several days. The only good news: Clark Air Base had excellent chow. I mean, this was *good* food, and I took advantage.

By the time I had been at the airport for forty-eight hours, I realized I needed some sleep. They told me sleeping quarters were available for transit military personnel. What they didn't tell me was that the sleeping quarters were nothing more than large screened tents with metal cots. I guess I thought the sleeping quarters would equal the food being served. But I was tired, so I lay down.

And then there was an oh-shit moment. All kinds of geckos were running up and down the inside of the screen. Another first. In Minnesota, we don't have those little lizards. I looked around at the others in the sleeping quarters. No one else was paying attention to the geckos, so neither did I. I was so tired.

After some sleep, I went back to the air base to check on the status of a military hop. The news still wasn't good. It looked like I would be stuck at Clark Air Base awhile.

I needed to get ahold of Sandra. She was at Floyd and Marie's place, but I didn't have their phone number. I called

Dad with the hopes that he could get a message to Sandra.

Well, little did I know that Dad then sprung into action with his political connections.

In the late 1950s, my dad chaired the Democratic Party for Chippewa County and ran for state senate in Minnesota. He knew then-senator Hubert H. Humphrey personally.

In fact, I remember handing out "Humphrey for President" flyers and campaign buttons at the Chippewa County Fair in 1960, when Humphrey was in a primary presidential race against John Kennedy. In 1964, I met Humphrey when he gave a speech at the Farmington high school for a Democratic rally Dad had organized. Humphrey was vice president at that time. Understand, this was a big deal for me!

So Dad called Humphrey, who called Clark Air Base. And guess what? He got me ahead of the line status.

But when the base personnel started looking for me, they had no success. Not knowing Dad was pulling strings for me, I had already decided to take matters into my own hands. I caught a military hop to Hawaii, then caught a commercial flight from Hawaii to California. It was $50, but money well spent.

In total, I had spent fourteen days of my leave stuck at Clark Air Base instead of with Sandra and Heide. That was a bummer after a long deployment.

Later that month, Sandra and I decided to drive down to San Diego to visit her aunt and uncle, Louise and Floyd. We were driving what's known as the Grapevine up the mountains when I blew the engine on our 1965 Chev.

Floyd and Louise drove seventy-five miles to pick us up in the mountains. The next day, Louise, Sandra, Heide, and I set out to retrieve the Chev. Floyd had to work, but he rented a tow bar for us to use with their new 1968 Pontiac Catalina, which was a big car. I hooked up the tow bar between both cars and hopped in the Chev, and Louise pulled me seventy-five miles to a repair shop.

It cost us $400 to repair the engine. We had to borrow the money from Lake City Bank. The Chev ran well from that point forward. However, when the engine was hot, the starter wasn't strong enough to turn the engine over, which was a pain in the ass. The car suffered this problem until I traded it in after I was discharged from the service.

Spring 1970

The United States had been sending combat troops to fight the Vietnam War since 1965. Tens of thousands of American military youth had been lost. The full-scale military commitment saw little progress in winning the war or defeating Communism. The Vietcong in South Vietnam, Ho Chi Minh's Communists in North Vietnam, and the Communists in Laos all absorbed tremendous punishment. However, the Communist troops continued to resist the United States and the democratic structure in South Vietnam led by President Nguyen Van Thieu.

In 1969, Nixon secretly authorized Operation Menu, a bombing campaign on and ground invasions in Cambodia. At the time, Cambodia itself was neutral in the war against Communism. However, North Vietnam was staging military supplies and amassing troops just over the border in Cambodia, with plans to attack South Vietnam.

Secretary of Defense Melvin Laird opposed the secret bombing. Laird saw little benefit, as did those on the National Security Council (NSC). NSC aide Richard L. Sneider predicted that the bombing campaign would only drive the North Vietnamese deeper into Cambodia.

But Nixon wouldn't listen. His administration went ahead with Operation Menu. They did not even notify Congress of the mission, as spreading warfare into Cambodia was *not* outlined in the 1964 Gulf of Tonkin Resolution.

This became another Nixon screwup—big time. Sneider's prediction proved true. The North Vietnamese pushed deeper into Cambodia, and the country fell into chaos. Prince Sihanouk was overthrown, replaced by Prime Minister Lon Nol.

On April 30, 1970, Nixon declared to the American people that US troops were to invade Cambodia, accompanied by the Army of the Republic of Vietnam (ARVN) from South Vietnam. It was an attempt to clean up his mess.

But without a long-range strategy, the incursion into Cambodia did little more than lead Cambodia to civil war and genocide. The bottom line: the destabilization brought forth the Khmer Rouge, followers of the Communist Party. As this party grew in strength and numbers, it overthrew Lon Nol's regime and began a murderous reign of terror. From 1975 to 1979, the Khmer Rouge committed genocide, claiming the lives of 1.7 million Cambodian citizens. Many were massacred and buried at "killing field" sites throughout the country.

In a 1979 interview, Prince Sihanouk said, "There are only two men responsible for the tragedy in Cambodia. Mr. Nixon and Dr. Kissinger." This is laid right at the feet of Nixon, who destabilized Cambodia. Declassification of top-secret documents and the Nixon White House tapes leaves little doubt—the prince was correct.

April 17, 1970

In the South Pacific, the USS *Iwo Jima* hoisted the *Apollo 13* Command Module aboard after successful splashdown. *Apollo 13* had launched from Cape Canaveral on April 11, 1970, for the third moon landing. But then on April 13, an explosion occurred two hundred thousand miles from Earth.

The next four days were filled with both terror and hope as the astronauts navigated their crippled spacecraft back to Earth, having never reached the moon.

October 1970

Our five months together flashed before our eyes. Before we knew it, it was about time to drive Sandra and Heide from Alameda back to Lake City—a long two-thousand-mile trip.

I requested a fourteen-day leave for the trip. However, the M Division officer would give me only a five-day leave. That wasn't enough. We knew it would take at least four days to get to Minnesota.

Unbeknownst to me, Dad called Humphrey—again. At this point, Humphrey was no longer vice president, but he still knew the channels and still had the clout. Humphrey called the captain of the ship, and the captain called the M Division officer.

Needless to say, I was given a ten-day leave.

My chief came down to the engine room to inform me of all this. He also informed me that the captain didn't like receiving a call from a former vice president. I told my chief I didn't know my dad had made the call, which was the truth.

On October 10, Sandra, Heide, and I began an eventful trip home. It was both sweet and sour. Sweet because the next time I returned home from deployment, we could begin a new life together. And sour because first we had to be separated for another eight months. We never dwelled on it, but it was always in the back of our minds: *Would we actually see each other in eight months?* We knew the dangers.

I remember driving through the desert of Nevada. The outside temperature was approaching one hundred degrees. I kept my speed to fifty-five, as I was concerned about the car overheating. I didn't want to be stranded alongside the road with Sandra and Heide.

When driving through the mountains of Wyoming, we came upon an early snowstorm. At times, it was hard to see the road. The snow accumulated rapidly, eliminating reference lines and the shoulder. There were cars in the ditch. I was driving by the seat of my pants.

I came upon an off-ramp to a truck stop and exited. As I pulled up to the gas pumps, I noticed the response to my turning the steering wheel was odd. I stopped at a pump, then realized I needed to inch forward to align with the nozzle. But I couldn't move—my back wheels just spun.

I exited the car and noticed that my left front wheel well was packed tightly with snow and slush. The wheel hadn't been turning at all as I pulled up to the pump. The other wheels were packed with snow too. As the car was filling with gas, I removed the packed snow from the wheel wells.

I had been authorized only a ten-day leave period, so we didn't have enough time to pull into a hotel and wait out the snowstorm. We had to keep going, and the only way to do that was to put some chains on the tires.

I checked out my tire size and went into the truck stop. Jackpot! They had a set of tire chains that fit my rear wheels.

Chains aren't the easiest to put on, especially when the weather conditions are miserable and you aren't properly dressed for a lying in the snow. In our defense, we had no idea we would hit a snowstorm on the way home in October!

Luckily, the trip only took one more day than we had planned—it was five days total. I had enough time to get Sandra and Heide settled before I had to turn back around and fly back to Alameda—and deploy—again.

Chapter 12

My Third Deployment to Vietnam

Flight deck officer signals for catapult shot of F-8

At twenty-one years old, I had already been deployed twice to Vietnam and had achieved the rank of second-class petty officer. As my third deployment began, I was now in charge of and responsible for the Number 3 and 4 ship service turbo generators.

I was qualified as top watch in the forward and aft engine rooms and as a section leader for M Division. While on watch, this responsibility included the supervision and direction of the assistant top watch, the Number 2 and 3 throttle watches, the booster and condensate pump watch, the lube oil watch, the bearing watch, the messenger watch, and the Number 3 and 4 generator watches.

Three years prior, I had just graduated from high school—and only with Sandra's help. Now I was standing top watch. I was responsible for the operation of an engine room of an aircraft carrier flying combat missions over Vietnam. Most important, I was responsible for the lives of the shipmates serving with me in the engine room.

October 21, 1970
Dear Sandra,

It was hard leaving you and Heide. All I could do was kiss you and Heide, then turn and walk away. I couldn't talk. Tears were running down my cheeks. I was a mess. I cried on the plane. My love for you is so deep. This was the hardest it has been leaving. I'm glad it's our last.

October 22, 1970
Dear Sandra,

The ship left Alameda and is fifteen hundred miles from Hawaii. It pulls in on the thirtieth for three days.

My friend didn't pass the second-class test. If he wants to take the test next year and sew on the crow, he'll have to extend his discharge date. The navy requires you to have one year of service remaining to be rated a second-class petty officer.

October 23, 1970
Dear Sandra,

I received a citation from the captain of the ship for

outstanding performance during my second deployment to Vietnam. Quite an honor!

October 25, 1970
Dear Sandra,
The captain was on closed-circuit TV and said the ship has a line period from November 21 to December 9, and then we head to Yokosuka, Japan.

October 26, 1970
Dear Sandra,
I have 199 days left in the navy. I'm counting down. I filled out my separation papers today. It feels so good. The navy is offering $10,000 to machinist's mates who reenlist for four years. I didn't even consider it!

October 28, 1970
Dear Sandra,
The chief wants me to join him on base in Hawaii and play tennis when we pull in. He told me he got a letter from an aft engine room friend discharged from the navy last February. It sounds like this friend has turned into a drunk.

October 29, 1970
Dear Sandra,
The ship pulled into Hawaii a day early due to a bad plane crash on the flight deck last night. It took out equipment used for landing aircraft. It'll need to be fixed before the ship pulls out for Vietnam. Four sailors on the flight deck were hurt. Don't know how bad.

As the LTJG landed his F-8, it hit the rounddown and broke into three pieces. The tail section stayed on the flight deck, and the engine went over the side. The pilot ejected from the remaining piece of the cockpit. However, the cockpit had tipped to the side, parallel with the flight deck. So when he ejected, he hit an armored hatch, bounced off, and then hit a fire truck.

What was left of him, they put on a stretcher and carried to sick bay. They found his head later that night in two pieces, lying on a catwalk.

They said that was his first night-landing attempt.

October 31, 1970

Dear Sandra,

My call to you from Hawaii cost $46.20—worth every penny. I miss you so much. I could hear Heide in the background talking. So cute.

November 2, 1970

Dear Sandra,

I heard there's a race problem in the PIs between the blacks and the Filipinos. The story is, seven blacks were killed and thirteen injured. They were all sailors. The navy has issued orders that E-4s and below cannot leave the base, and E-5 and above can leave the base but have to be back to the ship by 0000.

November 7, 1970

Dear Sandra,

Mr. Schmuck may have been an asshole, but he was an extremely knowledgeable engineering officer who understood what it took to keep the engine room operational and safe. The M Division officer now in charge is a lieutenant, and the junior engineering officer is an ensign. They both appear unseasoned, with no idea what's going on or what it takes to keep the engine room running properly. I'm glad I won't be here six months from now!

Mr. Schmuck and Chief LeRoy understood the importance of having thoroughly trained and qualified personnel to ensure mistake-free operation in port and at sea. We trained and practiced until we could perform our duties in our sleep. I believe the attention to detail of these two senior individuals saved the engine rooms from major disasters.

November 8, 1970
Dear Sandra,
Holiday routine, and there's smokers on the hanger bay—free hot dogs. Big shit.

November 9, 1970
Dear Sandra,
I received another smallpox shot and TB shot. My arm is sore, and the smallpox shot itches.

November 11, 1970
Dear Sandra,
The ship's schedule has changed due to the USS Ranger *breaking down.*
I'm writing this letter from station Number 6. It feels cool up here in the fresh air.
It's hot in the hole. We're standing a two-hour watch, and we come out soaking wet. That's because the fresh-air blowers are out of commission in the aft engine room. The fire main in the aft auxiliary ruptured and blew out the switchboard. So, fresh water can't be produced with the evaporator. The ship is pulling into the PIs tomorrow. Otherwise, we'd be on water hours. The ship's biggest

evaporator is in the aft auxiliary.

November 12, 1970
Dear Sandra,

We pulled into the PIs at 1600 today but had to anchor out—no open piers. The USS America *pulls out tomorrow, and then we can pull in.*

Only 185 days left in the navy!

November 18, 1970
Dear Sandra,

Due to the ship's last visit to the PIs, the sick bay line stretches to the fantail. The sailors who didn't use rubbers now have dicks dripping from VD.

November 19, 1970
Dear Sandra,

We're on the line flying bombing runs against the enemy. The captain ordered the ship on tropical working hours. Our chief leaves for the States in three weeks. There's going to be a big loss of knowledge and supervision to M Division.

November 20, 1970
Dear Sandra,

It's been a month since we pulled out of the States. It seems like a year. It's hard to believe I'm on my third deployment.

November 21, 1970
Dear Sandra,

No mail in or out. The captain came over the 1MC and said the ship is on a classified mission.

The mission was called the Son Tay Raid. Son Tay was a POW camp twenty-three miles west of Hanoi in North Vietnam.

This daring raid was a joint force composed of US Air Force Special Operations rescue personnel and US Army Special Forces (Green Berets), and it was supported by Task Force Seventy-Seven. The objective was to rescue as many as one hundred US military captives thought to be held at the prison camp.

The assault troops flew in six Aerospace Rescue and Recovery Squadron (ARRS) helicopters, which were accompanied by two C-130 aircraft from a base in Thailand. In addition, Task Force Seventy-Seven pilots flew a diversionary mission, dropping flares over North Vietnam; A-3s flew refueling missions; and F-8s flew missions for surface-to-air missile suppression, flight cover, close-air support, early warning, communications support, and reconnaissance.

But here's the kick in the ass: no prisoners were found at the camp. All the prisoners had been moved to Hanoi. Whoever was responsible for providing the intelligence screwed up big time. No two ways about it. However, if you read the military's official debriefing, it goes like this: "Although no prisoners were found in camp, the raid was a brilliant success in transporting, landing and recovering an assault force of 92 USAF and 56 Army personnel without a single loss of a man."

I have no doubt our military personnel carried out the raid with perfection. But the fact is, they were put in harm's way for a mission that was placed in motion before the intelligence was confirmed. It was another blunder by those who were wearing brass on their hats. Yet the military brass pounded their chests and gave themselves an attaboy for the "brilliant success."

As I look back, I realize the one person who must have been hurt to the bone by this failed mission was Admiral McCain, commander of the Pacific fleet. He played a key role in planning this raid in hopes his son John would be freed.

November 22, 1970
Dear Sandra,

A booster pump burned up in the aft engine room this morning, right before my watch. That'll have to be repaired as soon as possible!

November 23, 1970
Dear Sandra,

The bridge called man overboard. I need to muster in the aft engine room. Some guy fell over the side this morning, right before we pulled alongside another ship. The destroyer plane guarding the Hancock *picked him up. He's okay.*

The chief said the second class who left during the last cruise is going to school in Texas to become a state trooper. Both of these men have been responsible for my growth in the engine room. I consider myself fortunate to have served under them.

November 26, 1970
Dear Sandra,

This is our fourth—and last—Thanksgiving apart from each other. I can't wait to be home for a Thanksgiving with you and Heide!

December 1, 1970
Dear Sandra,

Standing four hours on, twelve hours off. A far cry from my first deployment with twenty-plus-hour workdays. I actually have time to think about home without falling asleep.

December 7, 1970
Dear Sandra,

Chief LeRoy transferred off the ship. I didn't get a chance to shake his hand. He'll be missed.

December 10, 1970
Dear Sandra,

In port in the PIs, and we're preparing for light off in the aft engine room. No problems, but it can be touch and go. I'm getting short for this shit. Personnel office is saying that the cutoff date for early-out is August 1971. So that would put me discharged upon arrival! Won't that be great?

December 12, 1970
Dear Sandra,

The ship is heading north for Japan. The outside air temperature is dropping, and the engine rooms are cooling down. The seawater injection temperature is dropping, allowing for a solid twenty-eight-inch vacuum on both main engines in the aft engine room.

December 16, 1970

I called Sandra from Sasebo and received bad news: my cousin Roger—Marie's brother—had been shot and killed in Vietnam. First Lieutenant Roger Anderson Jr. of the United States Army, First Cavalry Division, was killed on December 1, 1970, while on patrol in Phuoc Long Province, South Vietnam. The province shared a border with Cambodia.

President Nixon had troops in Cambodia without authorization.

December 17, 1970
Dear Sandra,

I heard B Division caused a black oil slick. They're looking for engineering personnel to respond for cleanup. I'm getting lost!

December 18, 1970
Dear Sandra,

Pulled out of Sasebo. My assistant top watch missed muster this morning and was written up. I went through boot camp with him, and we not only ended up on the Hancock *together but in the aft engine room together.*

I received your letter this morning saying the news reported nine men killed on the USS Ranger. *The* Ranger *has been having trouble during deployment, but no scuttlebutt on those deaths yet.*

I burned my fingers in the engine room, so my handwriting might be a little messy.

My research on these deaths was that a C-2A cargo plane crashed after takeoff from the carrier. Again, this was the same type of cargo plane I had flown in when catapulted off the *Hancock* on two different occasions.

December 23, 1970
Dear Sandra,

Thanks for the letter telling me about Roger's funeral in Montevideo. Very sad. Right before Christmas—it has to be extra hard for the family.

Two machinist's mates got into a fight in the compartment after liberty. It was bad. We let them fight because they were both drunk and too big to stop. The machinist's mate out of the forward engine room had his front teeth knocked out. The next morning, neither of them could see because their eyes were swollen shut. Both were written up for missing muster.

The navy issued Z-Gram #68, authorizing petty officers E-4 and above to keep civilian clothes aboard ship so they can wear them when leaving and returning from shore liberty.

This was meant to be a morale booster. However, it did very little to change the attitude and morale of those serving on ships deployed to Vietnam.

Z-Grams were issued by Chief of Naval Operations Admiral Zumwalt. In chapter 14, I'll write about a hidden enemy that took the life of Admiral Zumwalt.

December 25, 1970

Dear Sandra,

Our fourth Christmas separated, and my fourth Christmas away from home. Next year will be different. Christmas dinner on the ship sucked—no excuses for that garbage! When the ship is in port, usually the chow is good. If M Division operated the engine rooms the way they cooked the food, we'd be dead in the water.

The bridge just called man overboard. Some sailor must have come back drunk and fallen off the gangplank.

Thirty degrees in Sasebo. A nice change from the heat.

December 26, 1970

Dear Sandra,

Standing top watch in the forward engine room. Big difference from the aft engine room. Main control is located next to the Number 1 throttle, and the room is staffed with officers managing all engineering operations. They have direct communication with the bridge. I'm not used to standing watch with a bunch of officers, but no problem.

December 30, 1970
Dear Sandra,

Replenishing with another ship. The word is, a bag of mail fell overboard. There goes my Lake City paper and letters from home.

December 31, 1970
Dear Sandra,

I'm standing the 0000 to 0400 top watch in the aft engine room, so I'll see the New Year come in.

January 1, 1971—New Year's Day
Dear Sandra,

Happy New Year, my love! You know that bag of mail that fell over the side of the ship? Well, it wasn't really mail. Someone filled a mailbag with garbage and threw it over the side. A helicopter was launched and a destroyer was turned around to find it. The captain was pissed—cracked me up.

January 3, 1971
Dear Sandra,

The captain came over the 1MC and said the ship's crew will be voting on whether to go to Australia at the end of the cruise, before returning home. It'd delay stateside return by a couple of weeks. What a bunch of bullshit!

January 4, 1971
Dear Sandra,

M Division voted 45–25 in favor of going to Australia. I heard that other divisions were also voting in favor.

The ship went on tropical working hours. The third class who missed muster in December is standing assistant top watch for me. M Division didn't write him up for making it back to the ship late. The aft engine room is short on qualified assistant top watches.

Taking on bombs every day. We must need to blow up some of those Vietcong trucks. Glad I don't have working parties any more. Flight operations twelve hours per day and taking on bombs when not flying. Does the news report an increase in bombing? Nixon is bombing the shit out of them.

January 7, 1971

Dear Sandra,

We have a stand-down today—no planes flying.

I hear there's a postal strike in the States.

Congress approved and the president signed the Family Separation Allowance bill, which is retroactive to 1968. I'll get an additional $180 because I've been separated from you.

January 8, 1971

Dear Sandra,

The captain came over the 1MC and said a plane had been heading toward the Hancock *with mail but had to turn around because of engine problems. Ya, sure. He also said he wired higher authorities, asking about our mail and why we haven't been receiving it.*

Here's something interesting I learned: the ship can't go from the combat zone straight to Hong Kong because Hong Kong is neutral. So, the ship has to go to the PIs first, then to Hong Kong.

I'm standing the 0000 top watch in the aft engine room tonight. Standing four hours on and twelve hours off. I have the midnight shift every other day. Not bad duty. Plenty of sleep.

January 9, 1971
Dear Sandra,

Received my W-2s. I paid $339 in federal taxes. Only $2,585 was taxable on a gross of $4,218, so we should get all of the $339 back when I file taxes.

You wrote me and said that in five months we're going to start loving and living! I can't wait! It has been a long three and half years.

January 10, 1971
Dear Sandra,

The captain said the vote to go to Australia was 56 percent in favor. I'm very letdown. You'd think that after eight months at sea, everybody would want to go home!

January 14, 1971
Dear Sandra,

The third class out of the aft engine room missed ship's movement and was over the hill (absent without authorization) for fourteen days. He just returned to the ship. M Division is sending him to captain's mast. The old man will probably bust him from an E-4 to an E-3.

January 19, 1971
Dear Sandra,

Standing top watch in the forward engine room again. The Number 2 generator is driving me nuts. It has such a sharp whine when it runs. It goes right through me.

You wrote and said Heide's eyes are crossing and she needs eyeglasses fitted. I sure wish I were home to provide support and help you with her. I'm praying everything turns out okay.

An E-3 fireman was caught sleeping on the generator watch. M Division has restricted him to the ship when we pull into the PIs—no captain's mast. Staffing is short, and he's needed on generator watch. He was busted from an E-4 to an E-3 and thrown in the brig for thirty days last cruise. The old man wouldn't have gone easy on him.

I'm seeing that the crew in the engine room just doesn't give a shit anymore.

January 21, 1971
Dear Sandra,

M Division is holding a personnel inspection on the flight deck this morning at 0930. I'm schedule for watch, so I feel bad I'll miss this additional bullshit. Only 119 days to go in the navy, and I won't have to put up with this shit.

January 21, 1971
Dear Sandra,

The new Z-Gram #70 says the navy now allows neatly trimmed beards as well as sideburns to the bottom of the earlobe. I'm going to grow a beard.

January 26, 1971
Dear Sandra,

Lost a plane in the ocean today at 1800 hours. I haven't heard what happened to the pilot.

The following is a story of two pilots: one pilot who went home to his family and another who had his life cut short while serving his county.

The commanding officer of the Ghost Riders VA-164

attack squadron was on the angled deck elevator Number 2, firing up his A-4 Skyhawk. He applied external power, attached the huffer hose, and completed all the necessary control surface checks, but then his Skyhawk failed the prefight check.

The Ghost Rider in reserve was a naval reserve LTJG. The LTJG taxied his Skyhawk forward to the port catapult, hooked up, and went to tension. With 100 percent thrust, the LTJG saluted for the catapult shot.

But halfway down the cat track, the bridle hook catastrophically failed. The LTJG immediately pulled his emergency jettison handle to release the six Mk 82 bombs under his wings. There were six olive drag streaks on the flight deck where his bomb load slid across the cat track and over the side. The Skyhawk lost forward momentum and fell off the ship's bow into the sea, where it was run over and sunk by the carrier.

A-4 Skyhawk on elevator to flight deck

The LTJG did not survive the accident. Though this crash was technically classified as an "operational accident," it still hit home to the plane captains, ordnance men, and other flight deck crew who had befriended the LTJG.

January 27, 1971
Dear Sandra,

Good news! The chief of naval operations has ordered three-month early discharge for all naval personnel through August 1971. That means I'll be discharge from the navy when the ship pulls into the States—I'm short!

The USO is coming aboard the ship on the thirty-first with Miss Black America 1970 and three runners-up.

February 3, 1971
Dear Sandra,

Happy anniversary—three years! My last one away from home.

Sandra and I had been married thirty-six months, and I had been deployed twenty of them. And during my stateside months, Sandra and I had often been separated. I had to be away from home during underway training and when on overnight duty in port.

All told, we had spent less than a year together since we were married. It was difficult for both of us, but I'd never ask for it to be different. It cemented our love for each other.

On February 3, 2018—just days after I first wrote this chapter—Sandra and I celebrated our fiftieth wedding anniversary. Three children, nine grandchildren, and fifty years of love and fulfillment—we've been blessed.

Late January 1971

Sometime during this line period, an incident tested the extensive training and knowledge of those of us in the engine room. I don't remember the exact date, but I sure do remember what happened. It remains vivid in my memory.

I was standing top watch in the aft engine room. Main control had notified me that flight operations were about to begin. We were to stand by for a change of speed from all-ahead full to all-ahead flank. Not long after that notification, the Number 2 and 3 throttles received commands from the bridge for flank speed.

An increase to flank speed for the launch of aircraft meant the boilers needed additional water. Every steam-catapult launch required 250 gallons of makeup feed water. The assistant top watch and I were busy directing the booster and condensate pump watch to start additional pumps and adding makeup water to the de-aerating (DA) tank. We could see the water level in the sight glass starting to drop.

The ship turned into the wind and was cruising at flank speed (about 31 knots, or 35 miles per hour), ready to launch aircraft for another bombing operation. Then suddenly, a Russian trawler turned right toward the front of the *Hancock*, with its only purpose being to disrupt the aircraft launch.

Russian trawlers, also known as auxiliary general intelligence (AGI), were small fishing boats converted into electronic surveillance ships and deployed to collect intelligence for North Vietnam. They would notify the Vietcong of aircraft launch, intercept electronic messages, and collect garbage dumped from US ships to search for information. Another objective was to harass and disrupt the American carriers during combat operations in the Gulf of Tonkin.

A Russian trawler harassing the USS Coral Sea

Unable to make a course correction to avoid the trawler, the captain ordered an all-stop and then astern full. I was fully trained and confident on emergency procedures, but now the pressure was on. This wasn't a drill. This was real. In a situation such as this, a mistake in the engine room could be deadly. Everybody in the engine room had to depend on one another to carry out our responsibilities as we worked through this emergency.

All four steam turbine engines were now full astern. The Number 2 and 3 throttle watches in the aft engine room were dragging steam to 585 psi. The shafts and screws were now turning in reverse to slow forward movement of the ship.

These extreme measures had the old WWII carrier—and the engine room—shaking. My stress level quickly rose. Adrenaline was pumping. This was what we trained for. This was why we had trained all those hours that led to days, days that led to weeks, and weeks that led to months prior to this deployment.

The assistant top watch and I were very busy reconfiguring the equipment to respond to the astern operation. One important operation I had learned during my very first time at sea was to keep a close eye on the DA tank to ensure the water was correctly maintained. With the aircraft launch now secured, or stopped and with the ship's speed reduced, we no longer needed as much makeup feed water. Close attention was needed to ensure that excess water in the DA tank didn't blow the safety valve.

Just then, the Number 3 throttle man said the Number 3 engine was losing vacuum, down from twenty-eight inches to twenty-five inches and dropping fast. It was an oh-shit moment. The condenser for the main engine normally operated at twenty-eight inches of vacuum. If vacuum dropped below twenty inches, the main engine would have to be secured until I could reestablish and maintain the required vacuum.

I notified main control of my situation even as I managed the emergency. The assistant top watch and I focused on the gland seal. Gland seal was low-pressure steam introduced at each end of the low-pressure turbine. It maintained the seal between and inside the main engine's condenser and external atmosphere pressure. It wasn't a complicated system, but it used round mechanical weights such as those on an old farm scale in my uncle Ray's barn. Totally empirical and seasoned knowledge of the inner workings was needed to regain control of this antiquated system.

The vacuum on the Number 3 engine dropped to twenty inches. I had no choice but to instruct the throttle watch to secure, or stop, the engine and drag the screw as I notified main control of my situation. The Number 3 engine then fell to fifteen inches. The assistant top watch managed the weights on the back of the LP turbine as I reset the weights on the front. With each adjustment, we had to wait a few minutes, tapping the vacuum gauge, to see if the vacuum was increasing or decreasing. Those minutes seemed like hours. The pressure was on. The entire time, I kept main control informed of my situation, and they informed the captain.

The orders from the bridge via telegraph were now all-ahead two-thirds. The vacuum started to respond. When it reached twenty-one inches, I instructed the throttle watch to slowly open the ahead throttle and resume shaft rpm, as directed by the bridge.

As the throttle watch opened the throttle, the vacuum continued to respond positively. I informed main control that the Number 3 main engine was back in operation and that I was at twenty-eight inches of vacuum.

After about thirty minutes of an all-out adrenaline rush, I was soaking wet from sweat. But the engine room was back to full operation. Orders came from the bridge for all-ahead flank speed as the captain resumed launching jet aircraft for strike mission over Vietnam.

What's interesting was that I was never debriefed on this emergency in the engine room. They were probably just glad I didn't blow the damn place up.

So was I!

February 5, 1971
Dear Sandra,
An F-8 crashed today. He hit the rounddown. Most of the

time when the plane hits the rounddown, the pilot doesn't make it. No word on the condition of the pilot.

February 6, 1971
Dear Sandra,

Standing watch every twelve hours. I don't know what work is anymore. Unless there's a breakdown of machinery, my life is good—except for the food and sleeping with seventy stinking sailors right next to me. Making second class has not only helped with the money but has made my life at sea a little more comfortable.

February 7, 1971
Dear Sandra,

The captain came over the TV last night and said the ship is going to Australia for sure. A real pisser. The plan is to pull into the States on the third or fourth of June. I can't wait to get out of the navy.

February 12, 1971
Dear Sandra,

An F-8 came in low and hit the rounddown. It knocked his wheels off, but he didn't lose control of his plane. He gave it full throttle and took off again. With no wheels, he planned to try a belly landing in Da Nang. However, ten miles from the ship, he noticed his throttle was stuck wide open. He couldn't slow the plane, so he bailed out. It took two hours to locate the pilot because it was at night—but he was alive.

Word is, they never found the pilot of the plane that went down on the fifth.

February 14, 1971

Dear Sandra,

   Happy Valentine's Day! All my love.

February 18, 1971

Dear Sandra,

   Well, today I'm twenty-two years old. I have 105 days left to serve in the navy. I can't wait to get home. Three and a half years in the navy, E-5, and standing top watch—I consider myself a salty dog.

   The ship is pulling into the PIs in four days.

The term *salty dog* is slang for an experienced sailor, someone others look up to on the ship.

February 19, 1971

Dear Sandra,

   The M Division officer told me he recommended me for another citation from the captain for outstanding performance on this deployment to Vietnam. That'll be my third citation for outstanding performance!

February 22, 1971

Dear Sandra,

   The ship is pulling into Subic Bay today.

February 24, 1971

Dear Sandra,

   I went over to the base and took the written and behind-the-wheel tests for a military driver's license—passed. Whenever we pull into a base, my plans are to drive sailors from the ship to the main gate and make some extra money.

   One sailor taking the test got into the truck and started

maneuvering between the obstacles, as directed by a civilian base instructor. When the sailor was told to back up, he ran over several cones. If you hit a cone, you flunk the test. He got mad, put the truck in first gear, and smoked the tires as he drove back to where the instructor was standing. The civilian instructor looked dumbfounded as the sailor got out of the truck, threw the keys on the ground, and walked away. That was something to laugh about.

February 26, 1971

Dear Sandra,

We're still in port, and I'm standing top watch as I write this letter to you. The M Division junior officer (ensign) came down to the engine room a moment ago. He didn't ask what I was writing or say anything about writing a letter on watch. He was cordial, as was I. Those boot camp officers are soft on the knowledge of the engine room and have no idea how to operate it. I have more time backing this ship down than he has going forward. I'm short!

In that letter to Sandra, my attitude was showing!

February 27, 1971

Dear Sandra,

I was called down to the Number 3 generator to repair a six-hundred-pound auxiliary steam flange that was leaking bad. It took a lot of grinding and welding. I figured I'd do it myself, so I'd know it was done right the first time. My welding classes in high school have come in handy several times aboard the ship. My metal shop teacher, Mr. Johnson, would be proud of me.

Tomorrow, M Division is having a party at Dungaree Beach on Grande Island. I don't have duty, so I'm thinking about going.

Grande Island was on base, so sailors could go in dungarees to Dungaree Beach for R & R without being chased down the streets of Olongapo by Filipino kids with shoe polish. One time during liberty, I went off the base and into the town of Olongapo. A couple of kids asked to polish my shoes. When I said no, the race was on. They chased me down the streets. No, they didn't catch me. I was 150 pounds and very fast on my feet. I never went over again in the PIs. I didn't need the headache.

March 1, 1971
Dear Sandra,
Not much to write about, except I have ninety-three days left in the navy—I'm short.

March 8, 1971
Dear Sandra,
The ship is getting ready to pull out of the PIs tomorrow. I'm standing top watch 0400 to 0800 and responsible for light off for the aft engine room. I'll be able to hit my rack once the ship pulls out, and I'll have twelve hours off. My next watch will be at 2200.

March 11, 1971
Dear Sandra,
I received a package from my parents. They sent it the last of January. It took a month and a half to arrive.

March 12, 1971
Dear Sandra,

The condensate pump on the Number 3 generator developed a leak in the casing. The fireman and I had to remove the deck plates, crawl down into the bilges in the Number 3 boiler room, and dismantle and replace the casing gasket—a hot, dirty job. I'm mentoring this young fireman. He learns quick, pays attention to detail, and follows direction.

March 14, 1971
Dear Sandra,

On TV last night, the captain said the ship will pull into the States on June 2 at 1000. All personnel getting out through August 1 will be released upon arrival. Hot dang!

March 16, 1971
Dear Sandra,

Now that you've passed the written part of your driver's test, I'll have to provide behind-the-wheel instruction when I get home. Remember when I let you drive Dad's Case lawn-and-garden tractor and you backed it into my 409?

I went up to the personnel office today to check the early-out list. My name was on the list to be discharged upon arrival. My eyes were the size of saucers—I'm super short!

An F-8 crashed and burned today. Five men on the flight deck were hurt, including the pilot. He's still alive. He came in with the nose of the plane down. He knew he was in trouble, so he ejected, shot up, and hit the 08 level, where Snoopy the dog is painted. The pilot has two broken legs, a broken back, and broken ribs. He's in bad shape.

March 21, 1971

Dear Sandra,

Heavy flight operation—a lot of bombing runs. One chief joked to me that the government spent $238,000 on bombs and blew up a $129 truck. All these bombs dropped, and we really don't have anything to show for it but injured and dead pilots and sailors.

March 24, 1971

Dear Sandra,

Very poor mail service for being on the line. The captain's complaints about lack of mail aren't providing many results. How about this: sixty-nine days to discharge.

April 2, 1971

Dear Sandra,

The toilets above the M Division compartment were plugged this morning. (Somebody probably threw several rolls of toilet paper or his T-shirt down a shitter.) The pipe fitters were unable to unplug the shitters from above, so they came down to remove the clean-out plug on the main sewer line that transferred through the berthing compartment.

But they didn't wake and inform those sleeping before removing the plug. So shit, toilet paper, and piss suddenly blew out all over a second class lifer sleeping in his rack. He just shipped over a couple months ago—he's the dumb-as-rocks guy I mentioned before.

There's a third class on the top rack I was in boot camp with. He was sleeping too but didn't get any shit on him, nor did he get up. The floor was flooded with piss and shit—what a mess.

This was my chance to do a little heckling. I asked him, "So, how many years do you have left to put up with the

navy's shit—literally?" For some reason, he got pissed at me.
I have sixty days to go.

April 9, 1971
Dear Sandra,
The ship just left the line, heading for the PIs.

April 11, 1971
Dear Sandra,
The ship pulled into the PIs for repairs and some R & R.

April 15, 1971
Dear Sandra,
Tore down the Number 4 generator condensate pump—
again! This time I replaced all the internal parts. That's a big
job at sea. Had to have the machine shop machine several
new components. That repair will last until I get out, which
is all I care about.

April 20, 1971
Dear Sandra,
I went up to the personnel office and signed my discharge
papers. Inked my finger and pressed in on my new pink
Department of Defense ID card. I'm down to forty-three
days. I'm really short!

May 1, 1971
Dear Sandra,
Typhoon Wanda is headed our way, so the captain
secured flight operations early. We just broke away from
refueling our tin can (destroyer) and got word we're headed
for the PIs. The old man is trying to outrun the typhoon. The

ship is running at flank speed, and the engine room is shaking. Balls to the walls and full speed ahead!

That was my last line period. I'm on my way home now via the PIs and Australia—sounds so good. Thirty-two days to go! The ship would be heading home now if the vote to go to Australia had failed.

The ship was only on the line for six hours this month, but the old man said we'd get combat pay.

May 3, 1971
Dear Sandra,

When the ship pulls into the Alameda pier, don't come aboard. Stand next to the telephone booths on Pier 3, and I'll meet you and Heide there.

May 4, 1971
Dear Sandra,

The captain came over the 1MC and said the ship would leave the PIs a day early due to another typhoon. Typhoon Amy could add time sailing to Australia.

May 7, 1971
Dear Sandra,

The ship pulled out of the PIs, headed for Australia. Not happy—wanted to return stateside for discharge.

Going through a strait where Typhoon Amy was to hit. The seas are calm, and we're steaming at 22 knots.

My last letter to you will be May 18. The mail has been so slow that I'll probably beat that letter home.

May 10, 1971
Dear Sandra,

The ship is about to cross the equator and initiate all

pollywogs as shellbacks. Today was a big day for shellbacks like me. If I told you how many asses I beat and how hard I beat them, you wouldn't believe me. I never laughed and had so much fun in my four years in the navy.

At 0545, the shellbacks held reveille—and did we hold it! We have this first class who's been in fifteen years and is a grumpy old ass. Well, he was lying in his rack on his back, and a shellback came along and hit him on the ass hard from the underside with a two-foot fire hose. The first class raised up a foot off his rack. He was up and out of his rack in no time.

A fireman and I went up to the officers' mess, which is usually off limits to the enlisted, and we found our M Division officer and the junior division officer. They were eating good food and couldn't believe we were standing before them, ordering them to get on their knees. We made the officers put their pants on backward, crawl out of the officers' mess hall, and then walk to the M Division compartment.

Then we took all the M Division pollywogs to the enlisted chow line. They were serving some bad-looking chow—green shit. Once their metal tray was loaded up with this green shit, they were ordered to sit down and eat. No discussion. Also, they ate with no spoon or fork—fingers only.

We made them crawl back to the compartment on their hands and knees with their heads down, and then we made them sing songs. They had to do anything we wanted, or we'd beat their asses with the fire hose.

A garbage chute was set up on the flight deck, and every pollywog had to crawl through it. One of the guys shit in a plastic bag two weeks ago and put it in his steaming locker in the engine room for a while. But his locker stunk so bad that he took the bag of shit and put it under the water in the engine room bilges. This morning, he took the bag up to the *flight deck and threw it in the garbage chute.*

I also made those enlisted lifers and the M Division officer tell me I was short. They'd say, "Mr. Lund, you're short." I'd laugh my ass off. I could write another ten pages of our event—fun day.

Guess I'll start packing my seabag. Twenty-three days to go!

Please keep in mind that I wrote that letter to Sandra fifty years ago. Today, I view the equator-crossing initiation with a totally different mind-set. Having experienced this initiation as both a pollywog (see chapter 7) and a shellback, I can now say that humiliating and degrading another sailor was wrong.

Technically, each sailor could elect whether to participate or to report to a designated compartment for the day. But either choice led to abuse. You'd be severely humiliated if you participated or ridiculed if you didn't. I for sure would not want my grandchildren to have to make a choice between two such negatives.

One of the messages I've been trying to convey from the start of this book is that most of us who served in the Vietnam War were just teenagers when we were forced into military life, which is as different from civilian life as night is from day. In this atmosphere, young men such as myself were complicit in many different quagmires that would have shamed and horrified our parents—if they had known.

May 11, 1971

Dear Sandra,

They say Australia in May is like November in the States. So, if we go over, the uniform of the day is dress blues.

I had the 1200 to 1600 top watch this afternoon, and the captain decided to sound GQ at 1400. About 1350, the electrical load center in the aft engine room exploded—yes, again. A big ball of flame came out of the switchboard and lit up the engine room. Then no electric power!

No one was hurt, and no additional fire. But we lost all lights, ventilation, and electric pumps. All we had were prepositioned battle lanterns (battery-operated emergency lanterns), which made it difficult to reconfigure the engine room systems and equipment to maintain the ship's speed. All engine room watches performed as trained, though, as we scrambled to respond to the emergency. The engine room became very hot with no ventilation. I'm too short to sweat like that. I was soaking wet.

The word is, we're headed for a Japanese cargo ship hung up on a reef. It's about five hundred miles south of the ship's current location.

May 13, 1971
Dear Sandra,

I went up to the dentist for a checkup. He filled two teeth.

We went past the Japanese ship hung up on a reef. It was a fishing ship. The captain asked if they needed help; they said no. The Hancock *didn't even slow down.*

Garbage for chow today—what's new? They say you get three square meals a day if you serve aboard a ship. Three square meals of shit, that is. At least when at sea. The cook must not care. Maybe he's short, like me.

May 15, 1971
Dear Sandra,

I went up to sick bay for my discharge physical. I have a cyst on my left arm from all the shots in the same location. The doctor said he'd cut it out after we pull out of Australia. I'm sure glad I didn't have a hemorrhoid when I bent over for my rear end check!

May 16, 1971
Dear Sandra,

The M Division officer gave me special liberty and a day off for repairing the condensate pump. By getting that generator back online, I saved his ass from being yelled at. So with my day off, I planned to stand by for a friend and make some extra money, but M Division shot it down. The M Division officer couldn't figure out why I didn't want special liberty. They don't get it.

May 17, 1971
Dear Sandra,

Sandra, this is my last letter to you on this cruise. The next time I communicate with you will be our kiss on the pier. I can't wait. We can start loving and living!

Chapter 13

Returning Home: 1971

June 4, 1971: loving and living as a family

It was a long two-week cruise back to the States from Australia. The day before the ship arrived back in the States, M Division struck me from the watch list. I no longer had to stand top watch in the engine room. I was done. As quickly as my naval career began, it ended.

My last night on the ship, I lay in my rack, trying to sleep, but my eyes were wide open. Most nights on the ship, I was so tried I couldn't stay awake. But now I couldn't sleep. I was so excited to see Sandra and Heide the next day.

The ship moored, and the gangplanks were rigged in

position for the enlisted crew to disembark. As I approached the gangplank, I looked at the officer of the deck for the last time. Then I looked toward the pier. It was crowded with sailors' loved ones greeting the ship.

I started walking down the gangplank for the last time. The line of sailors was long, and it was moving slow. Eventually, I stepped off the gangplank for the last time and started walking toward the phone booths.

There were so many people. I couldn't see Sandra and Heide. But then there they were! Sandra with her warm, beautiful smile and long brown hair. It was the image I first saw at the entrance of Lincoln High School in the fall of 1967. And there was little Heide standing beside her mom, holding tight to her mom's leg. And then she peeked out, and I saw for the first time her new little glasses framing her face.

It was the homecoming I'd been dreaming of. For the last two years, I had crossed off the days, one at a time, on a small calendar I carried in anticipation of my discharge.

Ship's gangplank

As I look back, I have few recollections or memories of events back home from mid-1967 to 1971. These are stolen years. Nevertheless, I did make it back home to Sandra and Heide. Over 58,000 military families lost their loved ones. Sandra and I were so fortunate—we were together!

After many hugs and kisses, we proceeded to walk away from the pier. I never turned around to take a last look at the ship I had served with honor and pride for four years. Now, our joy was the future.

Sandra had reserved a hotel room just off the base. It was next to a Sambo's restaurant. I was looking forward to a good hot meal, relaxation with Sandra and Heide, and sleep—especially considering I had been up all night the night before.

We flew home, and Sandra's dad picked us up at the Minneapolis airport. It was the first week of June, and the weather was beautiful.

Sandra's dad dropped us off at our mobile home behind the resort motel where Sandra had lived during my third deployment. I walked to the motel, where Mom, Dad, and other family members were waiting. I hadn't seen them in eight months. Actually, I'd barely seen them in four years.

I sat down in a lawn chair in front of the resort with Dad. We looked out over Lake Pepin and toward the bluffs of Wisconsin on the other side of the lake. It was like waking from a dream.

It had been a long four years—I thought I'd never get out of the navy. There were moments when I had been scared, lonely, stressed, tired, and overworked. But it was over.

The next weekend was a Lund family reunion at Uncle Ray's farm, where I had spent my summers growing up. I had just come from my third deployment in a war zone where the USS *Hancock* engaged the enemy during combat operations. In four years, I had achieved the rank of second-class petty officer. I had stood top watch in the engine room. I had performed with distinction and had many stories.

But I never brought up my service at that reunion, nor did anyone ask. Truth be told, I never gave it a second thought.

It was June 2, 1971. I just wanted to get on with life.

Godspeed to all.

Chapter 14

The Hidden Enemy

USS Hancock *engulfed in toxic smoke after being hit by a kamikaze off Okinawa during WWII*

The USS *Hancock* was built and commissioned in 1944, toward the end of WWII. She saw battle in the Pacific and was almost sunk by the Japanese.

During the WWII era, many hazardous materials and chemicals were used to build military ships: lead, asbestos, zinc, mercury, polychlorinated biphenyl (PCB) compounds such as dioxin, and more. These and other chemicals were added to the paint, lube oil, hydraulic oil, glue, solvents, grease, gasket material, electrical wiring, insulation, and so on. These materials and liquids were present throughout the ship and had even a greater presence in the engine room.

The government knew the long-term health risks for sailors working in environments containing many of these materials and chemicals on the old WWII ships. However, the government turned a blind eye, as these ships were needed to serve naval missions into the 1970s.

Tens of thousands of sailors suffer today with health conditions directly related to their service aboard US ships built before 1970.

I'm one of them.

Asbestos

Asbestos is a very tiny fibrous material with the appearance of flour. A single fiber is so small and light it can remain suspended in the air for up to eight hours. It's fire resistant and slows the transfer of heat. It was used extensively as an insulating material in the engine rooms, boiler rooms, and other areas of the ship.

As a machinist's mate, your job was to repair machinery and equipment. This included removing and replacing the asbestos insulation encapsulating the machinery and equipment when repairs were needed.

I remember opening twenty-five-pound bags of asbestos and pouring this very fine material into pails of water. A brown cloud of asbestos fibers would rise up out of the pail. I'd wave my hands above the pail to disburse the cloud as I bent over to mix the fiber material with my hands. After I had a mud-like mixture, I would mold a two-inch-thick insulation cover around the steam valve flange I just repaired.

These very tiny asbestos fibers float freely in the air. When inhaled by humans, they lodge in the lining of the lungs. The human lung is unable to dissolve or expel the fibers. Over a latent period of twenty years or more, the fibers move to the outer lining of the lung, causing serious respiratory conditions such as pleural diseases, asbestosis, and mesothelioma. Mesothelioma is a cancer, and there's no cure. Once diagnosed, you typically have six to eighteen months left on this earth.

Unfortunately, I'm a victim of asbestos, the hidden enemy. I have it in my lungs. Daily, I take three types of prescribed drugs, including a steroid to maintain quality of life. If there's an upside for me, I never smoked. Those who smoked and have asbestos in their lungs have greater risk of cancer.

Remember Admiral Zumwalt, whom I mentioned earlier with the Z-Grams? He died of mesothelioma after retiring from the navy. He had served aboard many WWII naval ships. As a junior officer early in his naval career, he most likely inhaled asbestos into his lungs.

Medically, it's a proven fact that asbestos causes life-altering and life-threating diseases. It's also a proven fact that asbestos was one of the hidden enemies on ships built before 1970. The Department of Veterans Affairs (VA) should be proactive, then, regarding veterans' health. They should contact the veterans who served on the pre-1970 ships so they can get medical exams. Proactive screening could possibly reduce the number of lives lost to asbestosis and other diseases, and it could improve veterans' quality of life. I'm living proof of that!

However, the VA is completely reactive. The VA does nothing until a veteran experiences one or more serious health problems and submits a medical request for benefits. Worst yet, the VA doesn't provide any medical assistance unless the veteran can medically prove that he has asbestosis and also prove his asbestos exposure happened during his service aboard a pre-1970 military ship.

It's an uphill battle, and the VA throws up every roadblock possible to delay benefits. The appeal process can take years. The VA drags out disability claims with legal language and reams of paper that make veterans' heads spin. As it drags on, the veterans suffer medically and financially. Many times, they go broke and die before benefits are approved.

Here's an example: My brother served on a pre-1970 ship as a barber. Experiencing problems with his lungs, he applied to the VA for disability benefits. When the VA diagnosed my brother with pleural plaque, they used medical terms related to asbestos in the lungs, but at no time did they write the word *asbestos* or *asbestosis*.

In contrast, when the Mayo Clinic found an early stage of pleural plaque in my lungs, they used the term *asbestosis* in my medical report. Because of that specific term, the VA accepted Mayo Clinic's medical analysis on my behalf.

Of course, the VA didn't help my brother make a claim for disability benefits. Actually, when he made a claim through the Disabled Veterans Association, acting with power of attorney, the VA adjudicator denied benefits, claiming that my brother's rate (job) as a barber in the navy didn't involve working with asbestos.

It's true that my brother didn't have primary contact with asbestos, as I did as a machinist's mate. However, barbers in the navy aboard pre-1970 ships were exposed to a secondary source of asbestos. Without question, the sailors working in the ships' engineering spaces had the tiny asbestos fibers on their clothes and in their hair. The asbestos fibers floated freely from their hair and clothes and were inhaled by barbers during haircuts.

It is common medical knowledge that secondary-source exposure to asbestos still causes health problems. The VA should be drawing upon years of compiled evidence about asbestos exposure and then applying this evidence to future requests for benefits. Instead, the VA makes each veteran go to great lengths to seemingly rewrite the medical book about asbestos.

As for my brother, it has been three years since he first applied for disability benefits. He went through the appeals process recently, but his claim was denied again. They claimed he didn't provide substantial evidence that he was exposed to asbestos while serving aboard a WWII navy ship.

Agent Orange and Dioxin

Asbestos isn't the only hidden enemy veterans face. While Admiral Zumwalt died of mesothelioma caused by asbestos, his son Elmo died at a young age of cancer caused by Agent Orange. Elmo commanded riverboats in Vietnam.

Agent Orange is a chemical our government sprayed in Vietnam to defoliate the trees and kill vegetation in order to eliminate enemy cover. Over twenty million gallons were sprayed with aircraft. Dioxin is one of the main chemicals in Agent Orange. Agent Orange causes numerous health conditions, including some that are fatal.

In the early 1990s, Congress passed, and President George H. W. Bush signed into law, legislation providing Agent Orange disability benefits to all military personnel issued the Vietnam Service Medal. Across all branches of the military, veterans received Vietnam Service Medals if their service qualified under specific criteria. I was awarded the Vietnam Service Medal after my first deployment, plus I received two battle stars for my second and third deployments.

In 2002, however, Agent Orange disability benefits changed. Under President George W. Bush, Secretary of Veterans Affairs Jim Nicholson released a directive that only Vietnam veterans who had "boots on the ground" would receive disability benefits related to health conditions caused by Agent Orange.

That is, the benefits extended only to those who literally set foot on Vietnamese land—no matter how much time they spent there. "Boots on the ground" definitions also applied to so-called Brown Water veterans, those who served on watercrafts on Vietnamese rivers and inland waterways (such as Admiral Zumwalt's son). If you fell into these categories, you automatically received disability benefits for any health condition presumed to be caused by Agent Orange exposure.

But what about the Blue Water sailors, such as me? What about those of us who served aboard naval ships off the coast of Vietnam? Under Nicholson's directive, we were no longer eligible for Agent Orange disability benefits, and those receiving disability benefits had them forfeited. The only way a Blue Water veteran qualifies is if his ship docked in Vietnam and he went ashore, even briefly, to count as "boots on the ground."

I'm designated by the VA as a Blue Water sailor. Nicholson's directive was a slap in the face, a kick in the ass, a knife in the back, or whatever you want to call it!

The sad part is, eliminating the benefits for Blue Water veterans "freed up" funds for other VA programs. So the VA balanced their budget on the backs of the Vietnam veterans and redistributed the benefits to other sources. This pitted veterans against veterans, which is unforgiveable.

In 2017, there was a call to restore the benefits with the proposed Blue Water Navy Vietnam Veterans Act. It's my understanding that Congress wants to reestablish the benefits—but only by reducing benefits provided to other veteran programs or adding an additional closing cost on a VA home loan. Once again, this would only pit veterans against one another.

Here's the bullshit: Congress created the loopholes that allowed Nicholson—one person—to make sweeping changes to the Agent Orange benefits law. With the swipe of his pen, he eliminated the benefits for all Blue Water sailors—even though over five hundred elected officials in Congress had debated and approved the law, a president had signed it, and it had already stood for ten years.

The VA has gone to great lengths to justify why benefits shouldn't be given to Blue Water sailors. However, the VA spends very little to no time helping Blue Water veterans who apply for disability benefits related to Agent Orange. Like those applying for benefits due to asbestos exposure, each Blue Water veteran must prove his own case when applying for benefits due to Agent Orange exposure.

In contrast, the Australian navy has medical documentation related to the serious health effects of Agent Orange and has issued benefits to their veterans related to Agent Orange medical conditions. This includes those sailors who served aboard the HMAS *Melbourne,* which collided with the USS *Evans.*

The fact that the VA denies Agent Orange disability benefits to its sailors flies in the face of medical evidence. Statistics have shown a higher rate of Agent Orange-related health problems for Blue Water sailors than for military personnel who met the "boots on the ground" criteria. I believe this is because Blue Water sailors serving in the engineering compartments of pre-1970 naval ships came into contact with PCB-laden materials containing chemical additives similar to Agent Orange.

My Story

I'm a victim of the PCB dioxin. I have suffered severe health problems over the last fifty years yet was denied disability benefits related to Agent Orange.

As mentioned in chapter 9, I became very ill and was hospitalized just days after returning stateside. I was isolated and diagnosed with intestinal problems and finally released after a five-day stay. This was the start of an autoimmune condition that progressively worsened as the years passed.

After returning to the ship, I continued to experience mild intestinal problems. I didn't give it a second thought, thinking maybe it was from food or stress. I had more important things to focus on, such as being a husband and father, performing my shipboard duties, and advancing my rate.

However, after I was discharged from the navy in 1971, my mild intestinal problem progressed to severe. Treatment included a large daily dose of steroids. But the long-term effects of prescribed steroids caused other medical problems. After doctoring in Saint Paul and at the Minneapolis VA clinic, I needed a second opinion. In 1979, I went to the Mayo Clinic, where they diagnosed my intestinal disease as chronic ulcerative colitis (UC).

The only cure for my UC was the removal of my large intestine and rectum. I had no choice. At that point in my life, I could shit through the eye of a needle in a forty-mile-an-hour wind, or I could have my large intestine and rectum removed.

In September 1981, Dr. Beart performed a relatively new surgical procedure called an ileoanal pull-through. This procedure eliminated the need for me to wear an external appliance known as an ileostomy bag. Dr. Beart removed all my large intestine and my rectum, then built a J-pouch out of the lower part of my small intestine and sewed it directly to my anus muscle.

In the 1960s, this was called a straight pipe on muscle cars.

All joking aside, this was difficult surgery to recover from. A month later, I was scheduled for a second surgery to remove the temporary external appliance that had allowed the J-pouch to heal over the first six weeks. But three days after the second surgery, I became very ill.

Dr. Beart came into my room, made a few observations, then said, "John, I need to open you up." I remember he stayed with me as I was immediately transferred from my hospital room to the surgical center. Fifteen minutes later, I entered the operating room. The last thing I remember was being transferred to the operating table.

This emergency exploratory surgery was needed to close the perforation in the small intestine and address the stool that had leaked out and was poisoning me internally. I was hospitalized for thirty days—the recovery was long, painful, and difficult.

In the years following the removal of my large intestine and rectum, life presented daily challenges as well as numerous intestinal blockages leading to hospitalization. At age sixty-four, thirty-two years later, I required two corrective major surgeries. Both surgeries required opening my abdomen from my breastbone to my pelvic bone. Again, recovery was very difficult.

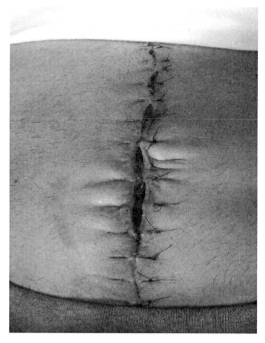

The long-term effects of serving aboard
a poison-laden WWII ship

I'm grateful for my current health. But due to my numerous disabilities, I consider my time struggling with my health to be stolen years. Stolen because the government knew that the chemicals and materials aboard the old WWII ships were harmful to humans. They knew the ships were literally laden with poison. They knew the chemicals presented long-term health problems. Yet the government chose to turn a blind eye to sailors' future health.

1. The previous picture of my gaping incision is bold and glaring. I want it that way. I want the US government—our elected officials—to see that photo and remember the following:

2. Years after they've left the military, *millions* of military

veterans suffer severe ongoing medical conditions—
including some that have gone undetected. Many
veterans need prosthetics limbs or wheelchairs. They
suffer from post-traumatic stress disorder (PTSD),
loss of lung capacity, loss of internal organs, loss of
eyesight, loss of hearing, and more. These disabilities
and health problems never go away and present daily
challenges to veterans. Worse, sometimes these
medical conditions are life ending.

Spouses and family members face daily challenges in their
endless care of the veterans. This experience is as profound—
or even more profound—than what the veterans themselves
go through. These loved ones not only care for the veterans
but also act as the glue that holds their families together. Their
tasks are demanding physically and mentally.

It almost goes without saying that receiving disability
benefits for my health problems was an uphill battle. UC is an
autoimmune condition that can be caused by dioxin, which
can breach a human's T cells. Dioxin was present in the PCB
chemicals that existed in most engineering spaces on WWII-
era ships, and the levels far exceeded parts-per-million
guidelines from the Environmental Protection Agency (EPA).

Technically, I should have automatically received benefits
under the "boots on the ground" criteria. As explained in
chapter 9, I was catapulted off the USS *Hancock* and flew to
the PIs via Da Nang on my way home for early leave after my
first deployment. I had my "boots on the ground" in Vietnam
for about four hours. Even that short time in-country should
make me eligible for VA benefits related to Orange Agent
exposure.

However, when I applied for benefits, the VA didn't
believe my story about flying off the ship on early leave and
landing in Da Nang—even with my letters to Sandra as

evidence. They denied benefits and my "boots on the ground" claim.

Researching PCBs used aboard pre-1970 ships, I found that dioxin was a chemical ingredient formulated within PCBs in the same way it was formulated within Agent Orange. When I reapplied for disability benefits, I included this evidence. It was the nexus proving I had been exposed to PCBs while serving aboard the USS *Hancock* and that this exposure more likely than not caused my medical condition, which had been written by a medical doctor.

These were the lengths I had to go to. Legally, the VA is obligated by law to help veterans prove their cases, yet they threw up every roadblock possible to prevent granting my disability claim.

Heather Vahdat, MPH, CCRP, has done extensive research on this subject, and she provided the following letter on my behalf:

> *Evidence of residual PCBs on* Essex-*class naval ships such as the USS* Hancock *and USS* Oriskany—*further substantiation that many retired military ships still present a significant risk of exposure to PCBs—is provided in a report published by the Centers for Disease Control and Prevention (CDC). The report entitled "Preliminary Survey Report: Pre-Intervention Quantitative Risk Factor Analysis for Ship Recycling and Repair Process" indicates PCB exposure as a potential risk for workers*

involved in repair and dismantling of US naval ships.

This report recommends that workers handling insulation on ships "don totally encapsulating chemical protective suits and supplied-air hoods under positive pressure. ... Level A personal protective equipment (PPE) is to be utilized when the greatest level of skin, respiratory, and eye protection is required" (US Department of Veterans Affairs, 2002).

If this level of PPE is required for protection from PCBs as much as thirty to forty years after a ship has been retired, it would stand to reason that at least comparable, if not greater, exposure risks were present when these ships were on active duty.

Based on Mr. Lund's exposure to various gasket materials, solvents, lubricants, paints, and insulations, I feel that it is more likely than not correct to assume that he was exposed to PCBs via inhalation and dermal means during his service aboard the USS Hancock.

However, given the confined lifestyle experienced on naval ships, particularly that of an engine room machinist's mate, I feel it is also reasonable to assume that Mr. Lund ingested PCBs through food and beverages consumed while in the engine and boiler rooms.

No Vietnam-era sailor was provided PPE when making repairs to a ship.

As the final nail in the VA's coffin, Ms. Vahdat included a picture of an individual wearing a Level A PPE suit, as required under the 2002 VA directive regarding the removal of PCBs. This cemented my disability claim.

We sailors serving aboard the old ships were not provided

any type of full-body protection and/or breathing devices. In the engine room, we were up to our elbows in lube oil, grease, solvents, liquid paint, and paint dust from removing PCB-laden paint with air-driven chipping hammers. In my claims for the VA, I produced reams of information from the internet showing the actual parts-per-million levels of PCBs in various materials aboard the *Essex*-class carriers, which far exceeded the limits the government has set for human contact.

The aircraft carrier USS *Oriskany* was a sister ship to the USS *Hancock* and was constructed with the same materials. In 2006, the *Oriskany* was scuttled off the coast of Florida in 212 feet of water as a tourist attraction for scuba divers. Before it could be scuttled, though, the EPA required that all PCBs had to be removed, which was a massive undertaking.

Now think about this. The EPA made the navy remove all but seven hundred pounds of the PCBs aboard the *Oriskany*, at a cost of roughly $1 million, because the parts-per-million levels of PCBs would have negative effects on aquatic life. However, the VA will not recognize the serious health problems PCBs caused the sailors who served on these ships. That's unacceptable!

The Australian government determined that sailors were likely exposed to dioxin via Agent Orange in contaminated seawater processed for drinking and cooking aboard the naval ships off the coast of Vietnam. Twenty million gallons of dioxin-laden Agent Orange were dumped over Vietnam. Yet the VA doesn't believe that a drop of it ever made its way out to the ocean. Keep in mind: the average annual rainfall in Hanoi is 68 inches, and in the mountains, its 168 inches. Of course, Agent Orange would wash out to sea via the rivers and contaminate seawater the naval ships distilled to make drinking water.

In research, the Australian government determined that the distilling process aboard its naval ships actually *concentrated* the parts-per-million levels of Agent Orange in the drinking water. The US ships used the same evaporation and distilling process as the Australian ships. However, the US government turned a blind eye to the Australian research.

Asbestos, PCBs, lead, mercury, and other chemicals— these are the hidden enemies to thousands of sailors who served aboard the older United States naval warships. These enemies don't kill their victims instantly; rather, they disrupt or change the structure of human cells, causing long-term health problems.

Again, the real kick in the ass is that the VA knows exactly what health issues these chemicals cause. Yet when veterans submit claims, the VA treats the vets as nothing more than numbers to remove from the files.

I'm one of those veterans. It took almost five years in a knock-down, drag-out fight with the VA, but I finally achieved approval of my disability claim.

Final Thoughts

Here's what's sad: my story, the book you've just read, can be multiplied millions of times. There are millions of veterans who were called to serve their country for what they thought was a noble cause in the 1960s and '70s. They too can recount stories of their military life that would make the hair stand up on the back of your neck!

As the real story of Vietnam continues to unfold today, it exposes how the corruption and deceit of a few impaired or ruined the lives of many. We know today that this cause was less than noble; it was tainted.

As the American people continue to learn the details of the past, they also learn about the struggles and hardships with which these veterans live today. On a positive note, Congress recently passed the VA Mission Act of 2018, which seeks to improve health care access for veterans. These new benefits will help ease the burden veterans and their families shoulder. We all are grateful for these benefits!

All that said, remember this: the most rewarding benefit is the priceless recognition of indebtedness the American people bestow on veterans. When you see someone in a hat or clothing that identifies him or her as a veteran, walk up with your hand extended and say, "Thank you for your service!" I can tell you, it's humbling!

And lastly, please honor the American flag. It's the fabric that holds our nation together.

Acknowledgments

To my editor, Angela Wiechmann: I realize editing is your profession. But honestly, I was often struck by the way you helped me improve this book. I would provide nothing but a vague thought in a few mixed-up words, and you'd somehow turn it into a vivid description. Without your reconstruction of my words, sentences, and paragraphs, my thoughts would have been lost or would have lacked intensity and meaning. You deserve the highest level of recognition. You did an excellent job, and I'm grateful for the time and work you dedicated to this book.

To Kris Kobe, my proofreader: Thank you for your diligent attention to detail and polish my story. You left no stone unturned.

A special thanks to Ann Aubitz, owner of FuzionPress: I was looking to hire a knowledgeable, seasoned publisher and printer – a person I could trust to provide an excellent product for a reasonable cost. You filled these needs.

About the Author

John Lund worked for Minnesota Mutual Life Insurance Company for thirty-four years and retired as the director of facilities management, and he retired fourteen years ago. He's an avid fisherman, on the water or ice many times each week. He and his wife, Sandra, reside in Rosemount, Minnesota, enjoying retirement and precious time with their children and grandchildren.

Barrier net capturing an A-4 jet

The third-class petty officer who trained me on throttles

A USS Lexington *Museum mock-up of the chow line*

The actual chow line

*It was 120 degrees in the boiler room, and I was on my
hands and knees shining deck plates with a wire brush.*

*Pollywogs who didn't listen—note the fire hose
in shellback's hand.*

Many lives lost and many more injuries in the explosion on the Enterprise

USS New Jersey

A bomb skipping across the flight deck—a close call

Sailors risked their lives to save other sailors and their ship, the USS Forrestal. *Note several heroes moving bombs so they wouldn't "cook off" and explode.*

Number 3 ship service turbo generator

USS Pueblo *at sea*

USS Hancock *insignia, which I view with much pride*

What Did You Think of *Vietnam 1967–1971*?

First of all, thank you for purchasing this book. If you found it interesting and intriguing, I would greatly appreciate if you'd recommend it to your family and friends.

Also, if you purchased this book on Amazon, I hope you could take some time to post a review. The success of this book is driven by the number of reviews submitted. Your support is greatly appreciated.

Please Visit my website at mmsnipe.com.